To Pe
Lov
                    ○ x ʃ
          26.06.07

Journey to the Centre of Your Heart

Celebrating 7 years of
a mended heart !!

'To say that Ray Bevan is a one of a kind is a complete understatement! Mark and I met Ray many years ago, and in the first 15 seconds of meeting him he had me laughing. Thus began a journey of friendship, of ministry, of great conversations about the joy and challenges of serving Christ, and of sharing many platforms where Ray sang his heart out, and then preached up an often hilarious storm, as he taught in his own way of the miracle of the faithfulness of our Lord. The reality of worship in the fabric of Ray's life has been completely inspirational, as I've witnessed again the kindness of God respond to the heart's cry of this precious man.

I am completely confident that this book will inspire and bless you. For these words have not only been laboured over, but lived through. This is a real life story of mountains, valleys, and the oasis that is discovered *only* as you are made aware of the awesome, and I mean *awesome* presence of God. So thank you Ray for pouring your heart out across these pages. And to you the reader ñ allow this journey to teach you, lift you … And I know you will also have a good belly laugh along the way.'

Darlene Zschech, Hillsong

'If ever you are serious about knowing what lies at the core of your being, then I dare you to read this book. It will cut you, and yes, you will bleed, but you will come out with a greater dependency upon God and his Word. I've known Ray Bevan and of his ministry for a few years now, and his passion for the things of God is truly evident in these pages. So, if you're up for it, bleed on!'

Pastor Bill Wilson, Senior Pastor & Founder,
Metro Ministries, Brooklyn, New York

'In *Journey to the Centre of Your Heart*, Pastor Ray Bevan lovingly guides you in exploring your heart condition. His openness and frankness about his own "heart" journey is a breath of fresh air in a world concerned about outward appearances. Through this book you will be ignited, challenged, and ultimately changed from the inside out to complete God's plan for your life.'

John Bevere, Author & Speaker

'This is a great read – a challenge to examine and reassess the vital internal motive to all we do in light of what we stand for as believers.'

Gary Clarke, Senior Pastor Hillsong Church, London

'Ray has been a great blessing to South Africa over the years, as one of our main conference speakers.

This book is not a doctrine of Ray Bevan's, but a reality of the life he has lived and learnt from over the past 20 years. This book will touch your heart and be a practical blessing to everyone who reads it. I highly recommend this book.'

Pastor Ray McCauley, Rhema Ministries, South Africa

Journey to the Centre of Your Heart

*The Priority of Maintaining
a Healthy Heart*

Ray Bevan

Authentic

13 12 11 10 09 08 07   7 6 5 4 3 2 1

First published 2007 by Authentic Media
9 Holdom Avenue, Bletchley, Milton Keynes, Bucks, MK1 1QR, UK
285 Lynnwood Avenue, Tyrone, GA 30290, USA

OM Authentic Media
Medchal Road, Jeedimetla Village, Secunderabad 500 055, A.P.

www.authenticmedia.co.uk

British Library Cataloguing in Publication Data
A catalogue record for this book is available from the British Library

ISBN-13 978-1-86024-608-1

Cover design by fourninezerodesign
Typeset by Waverley Typesetters, Fakenham, Norfolk
Print Management by Adare Carwin
Printed in Great Britain by J.H. Haynes & Co., Sparkford

Contents

Acknowledgements

Thank you, Alan, for sacrificially proofreading the manuscript at various stages. I do appreciate all you've done to fine-tune the punctuation and grammar. Thank you, Hayley and Alison and Marit, for having the patience to decipher my sometimes illegible handwriting and for putting it into readable type. Thank you to all the congregation of The King's Church Newport. Much of what is written in this book I've learned on the journey as I have sought God for food for you.

Dedication

To my wife Laila

I dedicate this book to my lovely wife, Laila. Thank you for being just who you are. You have been God's Word personified to me. With your life you have shown me God's love, God's passion for the lost and God's love for family. Thank you for your continual encouragement during the writing of this book and, on many occasions, being God's map as he has taken me on my journey to the centre of my heart. I love you.

RAY

Introduction

Both my parents could have possibly been alive today, if they had been more responsible in the care of their hearts. I know that during their generation, the awareness of heart disease and its causes were not as prioritised as today. The advancements in the study of heart disease and its prevention is way beyond what my parents would have had available to them. Triple bypass surgery, although still a major surgical procedure, is not so high risk as it used to be. The attack on cholesterol through diet and medication is reducing even the need of that type of operation.

Both my parents died of heart attacks relatively early in life, my father when he was fifty-nine and my mother at sixty-nine, ten years later. I believe both still had many years of life to live. In my father's case, decades of tobacco abuse took its toll. My mother had no idea about healthy eating, and as a result shortened her life by years.

Without seeming too dramatic, there are many Christians who live shortened destinies on earth, because they do not respect the importance of heart care – not just the physical heart but, more importantly, the spiritual one. Very often the condition of your spiritual heart can seriously affect the condition of your physical one. Some people may not experience heart failure through alcohol or dietary abuse, but could experience problems through bitterness abuse, unforgiveness abuse or pride abuse. Sometimes these things are just as dangerous.

We get so caught up in our desire to excel in many areas of our Christian lives, particularly in the area of gifting, that we forget that *as a prerequisite to God's choice of a human vessel for use, he doesn't check our performance but our pulse.* Some time ago, when applying for a considerable loan from our bank to build an extension to our sanctuary, I had to be subjected to a thorough health check. Because I was the senior pastor, and a major key to the repayment of the loan, they had to make sure my heart was such so I would stay alive long enough to give them confidence we would pay it back.

I had blood tests, eye tests, fitness tests... but the big one focused on the condition of my heart. The final examination found me wired up like an experiment, running as fast as I could on a treadmill, while the doctor gazed at the machine which monitored the reaction of my heart to stress. It was quite funny because after the test, which nearly killed me anyway, the doctor said no one had ever reached that level of speed on the treadmill!

'Why didn't you ask me to stop?' he asked.

'I thought I had to run on every level you set,' I said, 'because I believed that if I failed I wouldn't get the money.'

He laughed, because at top speed my little legs resembled that of the cartoon Roadrunner. They merged into a blur and looked like a rotary saw on full revs. The point I am making is, to trust me with such a large amount of money, my heart had to be examined, tested, and judged safe. God looks for people with good hearts. Hearts he can trust with his valuables. *He tests our hearts not our heads. He checks our pulse not our perfection.*

A sobering portion of scripture which needs respectful meditation is found in: 1 Corinthians 11:26–32: 'For as often as you eat this bread and drink this cup, you proclaim the Lord's death till He comes. Therefore whoever eats this bread or drinks this cup of the Lord in an unworthy manner will be guilty of the body and blood of the Lord. But let a man examine himself, and so let him eat of the bread and drink of the cup. For he who eats and drinks in an unworthy manner eats and drinks judgement to himself, not discerning the Lord's body. For this reason many are weak and sick among you, and many sleep. For if we would judge ourselves, we would not be judged. But when we are judged, we are chastened by the Lord, that we may not be condemned with the world.'

The Message translation of verses 28 to 32 presents the seriousness of irresponsible heart maintenance even clearer. 'Examine your motives, test your heart, come to this meal in holy awe. If you give no thought (or worse, don't care) about the broken body of the Master when you eat and drink, you're running the risk of serious consequences. That's why so many of you even now are listless and sick, and others have gone to an early grave. If we get this straight now, we won't have to be straightened out later on. Better be confronted by the Master now than to face a fiery confrontation later.'

Did you get that? 'Examine your motives'! 'Test your heart'! Why? For this reason, the text informs us – *unfulfilled destinies* … 'gone to an early grave'. Sobering stuff. My parents went to an early grave because of failure to respect the importance to care for the most vital organ in their bodies. Granted, much of their failure could be attributed to ignorance because of the lack of medical information.

But when it comes to the responsibility of Christians to test, examine, and judge their *spiritual* life pumps, we have no excuse.

'... Are you still without understanding? Do you not yet understand that whatever enters the mouth goes into the stomach and is eliminated? But those things which proceed out of the mouth come from the heart, and they defile a man. For out of the heart proceed evil thoughts, murders, adulteries, fornications, thefts, false witness, blasphemies. These are the things which defile a man ...' (Mt. 15:16–20).

The reason I felt compelled to write this book is to remind us all that God's Word read, believed and applied is the only safe medication to help us maintain clean spiritual arteries, enabling us to stay on this planet for our full allotted time. The human heart, unless we accept the biblical diagnosis for this unpredictable generator of good and bad in our lives, will cause us to continually try to rectify the problem with political legislation, social welfare programmes and self-help schemes or simply live in denial. We are like a woman I once knew who ordered a deep fat fryer. When it arrived through the post she excitedly unpacked it and tried it out only to discover it was defective. Believing it was a minor problem she took it to the man next door, the local *potcher* – a Welsh term for a 'jack of all trades (and master of none)' – only to have it returned in a worse state than before. Then she noticed a slip of paper pasted to the side of the box in which it had been wrapped saying, 'If received broken or damaged return to maker.'

We make the same mistake with our hearts; emotions don't respond the way we wish, thoughts run wild like a pack of angry dogs, and our lives resemble the aftermath of a medieval battlefield with broken dreams, relationships and sometimes even bodies strewn around our feet. We survey the consequences of a decision made while driven by bone-rotting jealousy, or what we felt at the time was a justifiable response, yet when analysed in the cold light of day, it was in fact all about revenge. Our hearts are sick, unpredictable and have the potential to cause human beings to do terrible things to each other. We, like the lady with the deep fat fryer, in an attempt to rectify something we know should function differently give our hearts away to *potchers*, professionals and pills, hoping they will solve the problem … only to discover our perceived earthly saviours are dealing with the same issues. Thank God for the Bible that not only correctly diagnoses the problem but invites all to 'return to Maker' to get it fixed. 'The heart', the Bible declares, 'is deceitful above all things, And desperately wicked; Who can know it? I, the LORD, search the heart …' (Jer. 17:9,10).

Believe it or not, it is this simple. God created our heart pure and innocent with a capacity to know him. Sin messed that up and he is the only one who can fix it. The realisation and acceptance of the divine diagnosis as revealed in the Bible is the first step to changing our lives and, consequently, our world. Jesus said, 'Those that are well have no need of a physician, but those who are sick' (Mt. 9:12b).

A four-year-old boy sat crying on the floor while his agitated father was trying to relax by reading his newspaper.

'How can I stop my son crying so I can have some peace to read my newspaper?' he muttered to himself. Suddenly, as he glared at the inside back page, his answer came. On that particular page was a scaled map of the world. So he ripped out the page, tore it into many pieces and handed the results to his son with a roll of tape. Then he encouraged him to put the mess of paper back together like a jigsaw puzzle, reforming the map of the world. The father was pleased with himself and settled down to what he thought would be a grizzle-free afternoon.

Within minutes, his son was tugging on his trouser leg declaring he had completed the task. The man was amazed at what he saw – he thought his son was a genius. The child had figured out how to put that atlas together perfectly.

'How did you do that?' the father asked, dumb-founded.

'Well,' said the little boy, 'on the other side of the page there was a picture of a man. I don't know how to put the world together but I do know how to put a man together. I put the man right, turned over the page and the world was right.'

What simplicity, what unarguable truth! The prolific writer G.K. Chesterton, commenting on what was wrong with the world, said 'I am.'

Accepting the biblical diagnosis regarding the condition of our heart is the first step in our walk of freedom. The realisation that only our Creator knows how to rectify it and satisfy our deep longings is the second.

God did not send his Son into the world to medicate the symptoms of a dysfunctional heart but to eradicate the disease. In the 1920s alcohol was banned in certain parts of America, but even though they tried to forbid the making and consumption of alcohol, legislation simply drove it underground. Drinking haunts sprang up all over the country; the production and sale of bootleg whisky was big business and rival gangs violently fought to monopolise this lucrative market. From time to time the police were tipped off as to the location of these illegal bars. They raided them and smashed all the bottles of the illicit brew, only to discover that in weeks these bars were again full and ready for more business. It wasn't until they discovered the distilleries and factories that produced the alcohol and destroyed the problem at the source that they made any real change. That is exactly what God did; he didn't just deal with the bottles in the bars, the fruit of sin – he destroyed the factory, the source of sin in our lives.

If we are going to live contented, fulfilled lives and also be a blessing to our world, there must be awareness that our heart is defective and must be returned to its Maker so that its longings and passions can be satisfied by a relationship with its Creator. We must also understand that the quality of our lives is dependent on the quality of our hearts.

The Bible says that 'out of the abundance of the heart the mouth speaks' (Mt. 12:34b), and even more sobering is the fact that the power of life and death are in the tongue. The condition of our heart affects the environment of our lives. With this in mind you can understand why God instructs us to guard it (see Prov. 4:23, NIV) because out of it flows the issues of life.

I once bought a house that contained numerous defects the previous owner had 'failed' to tell me about. The first year after I moved in was a nightmare. On the first night I decided to have a bath; I ran the water and returned ten minutes later ready to enjoy a relaxing, comforting soak, only to discover that if I had jumped into the water I would have been even dirtier than before I got in. The water was a rusty brown colour. I was horrified! I asked a builder for his advice and he told me that the inside of the water tank had become rusted for some reason and the only way to solve the problem was to use pure water to continually flush it until all the rust had been forced out. It was a lengthy and strenuous process, but what a joy to finally see pure, clean water come out of a boiler that used to be polluted.

In the process of life, our hearts become like that boiler: bitterness, disappointment, secret sin and a list of other things can rust up the inside of our hearts. God's desire is for you to enjoy the possession of a clean heart, loving heart, contented heart, so that what flows out of it can be a blessing to those around you. The continual intake of his Word keeps our hearts pure and, as we take this journey to the centre of our hearts, my prayer is that you will identify with some of the conditions highlighted and apply the pure water of life to the rusty corners that continually pollute the flow.

In his classic book *Journey to the Centre of the Earth*,[1] Jules Verne describes the adventures of a group of explorers who embark on an expedition to find the centre of the earth. The journey was full of surprises – the discovery of strange beings and unusually scary and devastating revelations accompanied many other shocks and scares. The characters found themselves crossing lava lakes, gazing at the skeletons of those from previous expeditions and the remains of ancient civilisations.

There is a journey Jesus wants us to take with him that is even scarier than Jules Verne's novel. On this journey we too will encounter strange beings, unusually scary and devastating discoveries and maybe even some skeletons. It's a journey we all must take if we want to be lovers of God and salt and light in our septic dark world. It's the journey to the centre of our hearts.

RAY BEVAN
December 2006

1

The Pouch, The Soil, The Heart

We all love reading the exciting account of a young shepherd boy going toe to toe with a nine-foot giant and coming out the victor. In fact, my last book, *Prepared for Greatness*,[2] is based on the preparatory nature of God, using the preparation of David's early life and how he was able to take out Goliath with a stone, a sling and a staff.

On reading once again verse 40 from that wonderful chapter detailing the account (see 1 Sam. 17), I saw something else that was crucially important to David's victory that day – a pouch: 'Then he took his staff in his hand; and he chose for himself five smooth stones from the brook, and put them in a shepherd's bag, in a pouch which he had …' David is a visual aid to how faith works and what faith needs to take out our giants – for the tools David used to beat his Goliath are the same as the tools we need to beat ours. Faith needs a stone, a sling and a pouch.

Satan is not stopped and pulverised with a testimony or experience, however powerful or charismatic they may be. David drew encouragement from past victories, and told King Saul how God had helped him in the past to take out a bear and a lion. Goliath may have heard all that but it was the well-directed stone that took him down. David was well prepared with specially chosen ammunition. He carefully 'chose for himself'. This was not a haphazard grab of the hand into the river for any stones. He gazed into the clear water carefully choosing and handling the ones he knew would be effective. The stones did not jump into his hands. He did not ask others to choose the stones for him. The lesson we all must learn in order to face and overcome our giants is: not only do we need well-chosen stones, but we need to gather them ourselves! You cannot live off another person's experience and you cannot fight with another's ammunition. You have to gaze into the river of God's Word yourself, and reach in with your own hand – that is, prepare yourself with personal Bible reading and study – and store a ready supply of divinely potent missiles. Jesus, out of the abundant supply of personally gathered ammo, stopped the devil in his tracks; not with a testimony but with carefully chosen stones from the river of Deuteronomy: 'It is written,' he confidently declared, and his Goliath was rendered immobile.

David also needed a sling. The stone was no good without propulsion. It needed something to propel it. It needed someone to aim it. Jesus declared, and with the sling of his mouth, hurtled the well-chosen word that stopped the devil in his tracks. There comes a time when something has to be said. The Word of God confessed is the sling that sends it to the intended target. Thinking the Word will not do it. Listening will not do it. It has to be confessed. It has to be declared. It needs a sling (see Rom. 10:8–10).

There is so much more I could say on the power of the Word confessed, but the purpose of this chapter is not to major on the stone or the sling but the pouch. The Word not only needs a sling to release it, but a pouch to store it in. David carefully chose the stones then placed them into a pouch hanging on the side of his belt until he needed them. Faith needs a storage space for the Word to be available for use when needed. Many ask faith to fight for them but when they reach into the pouch for the necessary ammunition they find none. Faith needs a stone, a sling *and* a pouch; the heart stores it for the sling to throw it. This is the crux of this chapter. We can major on gifting and how to develop our skill in ministry (the sling), we can boast of our collection of stones (the biblical information we have learned), but if there is no pouch to store them in, or if the pouch we have has been neglected, we will have nothing to fight with at the time of crisis.

The choosing of the stones was important and the skill with the sling was imperative, but if David had neglected to attend to the condition of the pouch, if there were holes in the bag, all his skill and well-chosen stones would have been futile. The condition of that pouch was as crucial if not more to his success that day than the choice of his stones or his skill with a sling. This principle runs right through Scripture. The stone needs a good pouch. The seed needs good soil and the Word needs a good heart. Before you read any more of my words, I would like you to pause with these thoughts in mind and meditate on the following scriptures: Mark 4:8; Mark 4:14,15; John 15:7; Colossians 3:16; 1 John 2:14.

While studying the parable of the sower, a simple but profound truth hit me forcibly. As I see it, the purpose of the parable is not to get us focused on the sower or the seed, but on the soil. The parable shouts loudly in order to get our attention to this fact; the condition of the soil determines the productiveness of the seed. The condition of David's pouch would have determined the outcome of the battle and here Jesus teaches the same truth through soil and seed. The condition of the soil determines the productiveness of the seed. The lesson is obvious and the reason for my writing this book. The condition of our hearts determines the effectiveness of his Word to produce a harvest in our lives.

Every week, I find myself standing before a group of people – if not in my own church, in other churches around the world – with a full bag of seed, sowing into a field of human hearts, knowing full well there is a difference between those who are listening and those who are hearing. The question we should be asking when receiving the preached Word as it is sown in our hearts is not 'Who is the preacher?' or 'What is the message?' but 'What is the condition of my heart?' You can have the best message preached by the most powerful preacher, but if the pouch has holes, if the soil is bad, if the heart is defective, you will never have ammunition to defeat your giants. You will never have seed to bear abundant fruit and you will never have sustenance to complete your destiny.

Through the parable of the sower, Jesus instructs and helps us by exposing three enemies of the human heart. These are illustrated by three different conditions of soil robbing the seed of the potential harvest.

The hard heart

Firstly, the hard heart (Mk. 4:4,15). Hard-hearted people are useless to God and easy meat for the thief of the universe, who easily steals the precious, powerful and productive seed of the Word; easy because it simply rests on the surface. We can develop a hard heart through a variety of scenarios. We can be disappointed with people, with the unfairness of life, and even with the God we fell in love with. Bitterness, unforgiveness, hurt, apathy and a host of other emotional and mental infections, if allowed to develop and grow, can cover the surface of our hearts with a hard callous that renders the Word useless in its attempt to take root. It becomes vulnerable to Satan's aviary. Irrespective of what has made the heart hard, the means of Satan's planned theft of the Word is varied. Here are some examples.

Satan can steal the Word through suggestion. Francis Frangipane, in his book, *The Power of One Christ-like Life*,[3] makes this interesting observation concerning Judas: He 'became a traitor' (Lk. 6:13–16). Judas turned from an apostle and a follower of Jesus into a person he never intended to become. Because he didn't regularly attend to the condition of his heart, he gradually allowed its surface to become impenetrable to the life-giving words of Jesus which were then easily stolen. I believe that it was probably through satanic suggestion that his heart became so hard and brittle that Satan could gain access at will until finally he could use him to commit the most infamous treason in history – the betrayal of Christ. He *became* a traitor. He was not born one.

'Has God … said' is still his line of attack. He usually steals the seed from our hard heart through our thought life. Our thoughts must pass through the sieve of God's Word to determine what is truth and what is a lie. For example, if the Word commands us to forgive but our heart has been hardened through bitterness and we refuse to obey, the Word is easily stolen and we *become* even more bitter. If the Word commands us to sacrifice for the kingdom but our hearts have been hardened through selfishness and refuse to obey, the Word is stolen and we *become* more selfish. If the Word exhorts us to serve but our heart is hardened through arrogance and refuses to obey, the Word is stolen and we *become* more arrogant. What area of your life is God trying to produce growth?

If you are facing the same test over and over again, it is an indication God is at work, desiring growth and maturity and development in that area. Ask yourself the question – what am I *becoming*? An honest diagnosis will reveal the condition of your heart.

Another way Satan steals the Word from hard hearts is through sight. He will try to steal the Word through circumstances. Think about Peter's water-walking feat, or Moses staring at an ocean leading 2 million people, commanded by God to go forward. What about the three Hebrew lads gazing into a fiery furnace hearing the frenzied shouts of a merciless king ('Make it hotter!'), or the 12 nervous disciples looking down at a piece of bread and fish in their hands and wondering, 'This is not enough to satisfy me, let alone this hungry crowd!'? How many seeds of faith have been stolen from hard hearts of unbelief because they have allowed the pressure of circumstances to overwhelm them? Don't allow the devil to intimidate you through seemingly impossible circumstances. If you are facing one right now – rejoice! It could be an indication that Satan fears the result of your faith in that word God is sowing in your heart.

The third way Satan steals the Word through our heart is through people. Satan will attempt to steal the Word from taking root in your heart through someone in your close circle of friendship – even, possibly, someone in your own family. Peter was riding high after receiving commendation from Jesus because of his sensitivity to hear from heaven. 'Who do men say that I am?' Jesus asked (Mk. 8:27). After a couple of failed attempts by some of the other disciples, Peter was placed top of the class with his world-famous answer: 'You are the Christ, the Son of the living God' (Mt. 16:16). Jesus then changed the tone of the conversation as he explained to his disciples the real purpose of his mission – to be rejected, to suffer and be killed. Peter, still heady from receiving his spiritual Oscar, began to rebuke Jesus for spreading negativity amongst the team. After all, he was the one who could hear from heaven; his advice was sound! His advice could be relied upon! Jesus immediately recognised Satan's attempt to steal the word of destiny from one of his closest friends. Even though Jesus was generous in his encouragement to Peter, when he recognised Peter was being used as a tool of Satan to steal the Word, Jesus was uncompromising in his rebuke: 'Get behind Me, Satan! You are an offence to Me, for you are not mindful of the things of God, but the things of men' (Mt. 16:23).

I'm sure Peter stood open-mouthed, asking himself the question, 'Was it something I said?' Even with his closest associates, Jesus realised the potential in them to sidetrack his purpose. Jesus' heavenly purpose was more important to him than his earthly relationships. Hard-hearted people who value earthly relationships above heavenly purpose are vulnerable for hell's thief, because they have no clear kingdom purpose and no strong biblical conviction. They are addicted to praise and, because they are controlled by the lust to be liked, people can easily influence them.

The shallow heart

The second condition of the heart highlighted in the parable of the sower is the shallow heart (Mk: 4:5,6,16,17). The problem here was not hardness but the depth. Jesus explained a problem arose 'because it had no depth'. Jesus did not oversell the gospel or try some attractive sales pitch to lure customers. It wasn't: 'Buy one, get one free!' Jesus promised to take away our sin, not our hardship. I say this because so many people live with an attitude of complaint because life is too tough. They were promised a happy life if they received Christ and now believe they were lied to because of the discovery of possibly added problems connected to their relationship with him. We must be careful, in our enthusiasm to persuade someone to make a decision, that we don't oversell the gospel.

Understanding why trials, temptations and hardship are allowed by God to be a part of our lives will save us from much disappointment. He's after depth. A good harvest cannot be produced from shallow ground. James comes to our aid with his revelation concerning our trials of life (Jas. 1:2,3) – 'knowing' this. Very often, when you know the 'why' you can endure any 'what'. Jesus never deceived us concerning the difficulties connected to serving him (Jn. 16:33). F.B. Meyer said that if he was told that he was in for a hard journey, every hard jolt along the way reminded him that he was on the right road! The late nineteenth-century preacher Charles Spurgeon said that great hearts could only be made through great troubles and I really love what Billy Graham said on this subject – that mountain-tops are for views and inspiration but it is in the valleys that fruit is grown.[4] God is after character; he's after a depth of soil he knows can accommodate the type of fruit he is after.

Great character is the cumulative result when great pain and disappointment intersect a person with a teachable spirit. Crisis does not develop character, it simply reveals it. That is why leaders emerge during times of crisis; because they have allowed the tough times to develop them and deepen them. It has been said that rich character is the soil for which God searches when producing his harvest of deliverance both for an individual and for a nation.[5] At 56 years of age, Winston Churchill lay in a hospital bed in Canada after being knocked down by a bus. His political career was seemingly at an end after being kicked out of his government's cabinet. The wealth he inherited from his family had been lost through unfortunate financial circumstances. He was depressed, lonely and at that point felt worthless and useless. Just a few years later a crisis arose in the form of a Chaplin-moustached tyrant called Hitler who threatened the democracy and human right of every individual in Europe. As Churchill stood before the door of 10 Downing Street, having been called upon in this hour of crisis to lead our nation in its greatest hour of trial, he was able to recall that he felt as if he was walking with destiny; that all his life had been preparation for that moment. His life, he felt, had been prepared for that hour of trial.

If you are tempted to react with anger against the adverse circumstances in your life – think again. God is looking for soil with depth to produce a harvest to bless thousands. That soil could be cultivating in your heart right now. Be encouraged with the words of Peter: 'In this you greatly rejoice, though now for a little while, if need be, you have been grieved by various trials, that the genuineness of your faith, being much more precious than gold that perishes, though it is tested by fire, may be found to praise, honour, and glory at the revelation of Jesus Christ' (1 Pet. 1:6,7).

The neglected heart

The third heart condition that disables the power of God's Word in our lives is found in Mark 4:17–19 – the neglected heart. If Satan cannot steal the Word from hard hearts, if trial, persecution and hardship are futile in their attempt to prevent depth, then the third enemy will execute its plan – sabotage through distraction. Distraction's assault will come in the form of a three-wave attack. Firstly, the temptation to worry ('the cares of this world'); secondly, the temptation to want ('the deceitfulness of riches'); and thirdly, the temptation to wander ('the desires for other things').

While we give in to these carrots dangled daily before us, we take our eyes off the Shepherd who has promised to lovingly and faithfully lead us, protect us and provide for us. We begin to focus on worry, wants and wanderings until the seed full of divine potential is completely overwhelmed and incapacitated. Discouragement is the killer of passion. Presumption is the seed of familiarity. Negativity is the polluter of vision. Fear paralyses potential. Laziness is the thief of life, and distraction is the prostitute of Satan. Don't be deceived by her seduction.

Finally ...

The Pouch, The Soil, The Heart – their condition is imperative to the success of our lives. What is the condition of yours?

2

Visitation of Violence

When it comes to his temple, the place where God desires to meet with his people, whether it is a crude portable structure carried around in the Sinai desert, the elaborate temples of Solomon and Zerubbabel, or his present dwelling place, the human heart, God is particular and passionate about the condition of his house.

On one occasion, Jesus stunned and shocked a whole crowd of people as he stormed around their workplace with a home-made whip, angrily trashing the place and shouting strong words of rebuke to those who had been responsible for turning this particular establishment into a 'den of thieves' (see Mt. 21:12,13). The place was the temple in Jerusalem; the people were the custodians, and the problem was that Jesus didn't like the party!

Imagine coming home to your house, having been promised by your son that the place would be looked after, only to find it full of teenage drunks throwing up all over your furniture, writing their names on the walls, having sex in your bed and totally disrespecting the fact the house belongs to someone else. Intensify that a million times and you may get a greater understanding of how Jesus felt that day when he arrived at his Father's house to find worse. The people who were supposed to make sure the Father's house – the place where he met with his people – was kept pure in its practice and purpose, had turned it into a three-ring circus. This wasn't just a case of neglect but of wilful abuse of something holy that had been entrusted to them.

God no longer dwells in temples made with hands but human hearts and his passion for purity is still the same. He still wants a clean house. The whole procedure laid down in the Old Testament for approaching God was meticulous. The reason was not because God was finicky about detail, but that he was passionate about purity. Later I will be devoting a chapter to the invaluable qualities of a pure heart. But for now, come with me as we investigate in more detail this incident in Jesus' ministry referred to by commentators as 'The Cleansing of the Temple' and discover that what Jesus did there in Jerusalem 2,000 years ago, he desires to do today in every house that he inhabits.

Do you sense occasionally there are seasons in your life when civil war seems to be breaking out in your heart – unproductive habits that previously never bothered you are now being scrutinised by a highly sensitised conscience? Do you sense unChristlike attitudes being attacked from the inside: ungodly, unprofitable, unnecessary things pertaining to your lifestyle being exposed by the light of God's Word? Do you walk away from a conversation after listening to gossip, or sharing it, and feel ashamed, whereas before you felt justified? Do you feel like you've betrayed your best friend as you listen to the laughter of your workmates because of the dirty joke you've just told them? Do you feel disgusted with yourself after watching a stranger undress in the corner of your living room, or after observing a couple you've never met having sex, whereas before you classed it as entertainment? Does sleep evade you at night because you had to cover up and deceive to get your own way? If you have honestly answered 'yes' to some or most in that list, don't be discouraged; in fact rejoice because you are experiencing what I call a visitation of violence. Your heart is his temple and he wants it to be what he intended it to be, a house decorated with purity, furnished with prayer and fuelled with passion.

When it comes to how he wants his house, the Holy Spirit does not come with a list of preferences but a declaration of requirements. He does not come to negotiate optional extras but to stipulate clearly the conditions for occupancy. God is violently visiting his temple. He wants it back, restored to what he originally intended it to be. In order for this to happen, he needs to overturn some tables and drive out some impostors.

Jesus has come under heavy criticism from many unbelieving critics because of his behaviour that day, but that is simply down to their ignorance of a loving God concerned and responsible for those he loves and for what he owns. The events that took place that day in the temple were not the manifestations of an uncontrolled reactionary God, but of a premeditated course of action based on accurate information fuelled by Godly jealous love. This was not the first time Jesus had visited the scene. He had already checked the place out. Mark teaches us that along with his disciples on a previous visit, he had gone into the temple 'looked around surveying and observing everything' (Mk. 11:11, Amplified version). Then he went to Bethany and from there came riding on a donkey to the praises of the multitudes … with a whip in his hand. While everyone was caught up with the external spectacular, Jesus was heading for the temple to put things straight.

Sometimes, we pat ourselves on the back for the way we welcome Jesus with our praise and shout his name in honour with our lips. But he is more interested in the condition of our hearts rather than the melody of our songs. While we get caught up with the mechanics of praise and the melody of the praise song, Jesus is weighing the motive. Sometimes I feel we treat the use of worship songs like the current pop charts: 'We don't sing that song any more, that's out now!' While we critique, analyse or rave over the latest praise song, heaven observes and applauds some persecuted Christian quietly singing a sacrifice of praise while being beaten for their lack of compromise. Let's be careful not to put on a pedestal the style, the structure or the songwriter, and just try to remember *who* we're seeking to worship.

To understand more clearly how God actually wants us to co-operate with him as he seeks to take us on a journey to the centre of our heart, we can see in this picture of Jesus cleansing the temple two important aspects of God's procedure in his desire to clean the house.

The motive

Firstly, the motive; quoting the words God gave to Jeremiah, who was commanded to declare judgement on a disobedient people, Jesus clearly reveals the motive behind his actions (see also Is. 56:7): 'It is written,' Jesus thundered. 'My house ...' Not *your* house or *our* house, but *my* house. I can't imagine any father coming home to a house trashed by his teenage children and saying, 'Well you have just as much right as I do. Do as you want in this house, it's as much yours as mine!' That may be true as long as the children live within the boundaries set by the parents, but when those boundaries are breached they receive a painful reminder concerning two things –

parenting and ownership. The father enters that house and rectifies the situation based on his parental rights and his ownership rights. He pays the mortgage and the children are the fruit of his loins! When it comes to confronting and rearranging the mess in our lives, God does it based on the same two principles – parental rights and ownership rights. Your heart is his house and you are his child. You were conceived by the power of his Spirit and your body is now the temple of the Holy Spirit. He is both redeemer and relative, Father and Lord.

Any father who would allow his children to do as they wish in the family home lacks both responsibility and love. God lacks neither. He is not irresponsible concerning what he paid for and who he conceived. His relationship to us is both Lord and Father and his motive for sometimes seemingly violent action concerning our behaviour is based on that premise. God will sometimes find it necessary to deal with us violently – but never viciously. The difference between the two words is *motive*. God sent his living Word into his house with such force because his desire was to protect and preserve something that was precious to him. He loves you too much to leave you as you are and he has invested too much in you to see you destroyed.

When he deals with us in his way it can sometimes be very painful but in hindsight we realise it was very profitable. C.S. Lewis said that pain was God's megaphone. Rick Warren in his wonderful book *The Purpose Driven Life*[6] puts it like this:

> Pain is God's way of arousing us from spiritual lethargy, your problems are not punishment they are a wake-up call from God. God is not mad at you He is mad about you and He will do whatever it takes to bring you back into fellowship with Him.

When God took up residence in your life, he had no intention of sharing it with any other tenants. 'You are my house,' he declares. 'I have bought you with a price too high for anyone else to pay. I have a right as a parent and house owner to correct and adjust as necessary.' It's good for us to continually remind ourselves we are not our own, we are his.

The mission

The second thing I noticed about Jesus' violent visit to the temple was his mission. He was not out of control, ranting and raving with his emotions and actions uncoordinated, he was on a mission; he knew exactly where he was and what he had to do. 'Then Jesus went into the temple of God and drove out all those who bought and sold in the temple, and overturned the tables of the money changers and the seats of those who sold doves' (Mt. 21:12).

Jesus, after surveying the scene with divinely inspired scrutiny, realised nothing less than drastic action was needed to make a statement concerning God's purity and God's order. He does exactly the same with our hearts; the word used for this ongoing process in our lives is 'sanctification' – the process by which the Holy Spirit desires to make us like Jesus. I could never understand Hebrews 10:14 until I understood this aspect of the work carried out by the Holy Spirit: 'For … he perfected forever all those whom he is making holy' (NLT). It sounds strange, how can you perfect that which has already been declared perfect? How can you make holy that which has already been pronounced holy? The principle of the jigsaw puzzle can help us here. You look down at an assortment of uncoordinated, unconnected, irregular-shaped pieces of cardboard and wonder, where do I start? How can this mess produce something that brings pleasure to the eye?

The answer is simple; look at the picture on the top of the box and you will see the desired result. God has already taken the picture of your destiny; we are already complete in him. He knows what he wants us to look like – his Son Jesus. And he knows what he created us to do – our destiny. Rick Warren puts it like this:

> God was thinking about you long before you were thinking about Him. His purpose for your life predates your conception. He planned it before you existed without your input. You may choose your career, your spouse, your hobbies and many other parts of your life but you don't choose your purpose.

God's mission concerning you is to make you what he's already designed you to be. That's why he is ruthless and determined about the centre of operations, your heart, because that is where the process begins and ends.

God showed me something quite sobering related to Jesus' action in the temple that day; something that every believer needs to grasp. So let's read Matthew 21:12 again: 'Then Jesus went into the temple of God and drove out all those who bought and sold in the temple, and overturned the tables of the money changers and seats of those who sold doves.' This verse gives us insight into Jesus' attitude, and also the target of his discipline.

He 'drove out' – there was no negotiation of terms before expulsion or settlement through an easy payment plan. He was very specific as to where he channelled his righteous anger: the tables of the money changers and the seats of those who sold doves. When I saw what I am about to share with you, I began to understand why Jesus was so aggravated. Tables represent agenda. 'Let's get everything on the table' is a phrase we hear often to describe the desire for everyone participating in a business deal or some other venture where trust is essential: it is to be honest, to be transparent, to bring out of hiding any hidden agenda that could jeopardise the project. Jesus kicked over the tables; he kicked over their agendas, polluted motives and double standards. They were the focus of his righteous gaze and the target for his violent feet.

The seats of the dove sellers were next. A seat represents ownership. The ministry God has given me involves travelling all over the world and flying on lots of planes. Sometimes after sitting in what I believe to be my allocated seat, someone comes along, looks at their boarding pass and says, 'Excuse me, I think you're sitting in my seat.' I check my boarding pass and sure enough I am sitting in the wrong seat and have to move. The scripture says Jesus came into the temple and overturned 'the seats of those who sold doves'. The dove is a representation of the Holy Spirit, the seats represent ownership, and the tables represent agenda – what does this mean for us? To summarise, I believe this is a perfect picture of Jesus' displeasure of a Christian sitting in the seat of ownership over a gift given them by God … with a hidden agenda. Jesus comes along like the person on the plane and says, 'Excuse me, I think you're sitting in my seat.' If we refuse to move he simply kicks the seat out from under us and exposes our hidden agenda.

The seats of the dove sellers and tables of money changers fill our churches and defile our hearts. Here we have a perfect picture of a Christian refusing to use their God-given gifting to bless the church and the world because the price isn't right. They believe they own that gift and their agenda is, 'I will bless you with my gift, *if …*' The issue was not the money or the doves, it was the buying and selling, trading God-given holy things designed to be a blessing, not to be bought and sold for the best price.

There is a spiritual prostitution taking place on a mass scale in the body of Christ. 'I will bless you with my gift if the price is right' – exorbitant financial demands from ministries and preachers before they will accept an invitation to bless a group of people with their gift! Plausible reasons are given to justify their demands, mainly the rising cost of their ministry etc. but Jesus never said, 'I will build your ministry.' He said, 'I will build My church' (Mt. 16:18). We need to continually allow the Holy Spirit to examine our hearts as to agenda and ownership. Are our financial arrangements and requirements needed to maintain our image or build his kingdom? Our hearts are deceitful and sometimes the lines can be blurred. Jesus is visiting his temple to overturn agendas and the seat of ownership.

Bringing this down to a local church level, the dove sellers and money changers are those Christians who say, 'I will bless you with my gift if I agree with the leadership. I'm not serving in this church until the leadership sees my point of view. Until then I'm going to withhold my tithes and service.' They are dove sellers sitting in a place of ownership with a hidden agenda. Jesus has come to drive out that attitude and claim his seat.

'I will bless you with my gift if I receive my due recognition; my gift deserves a higher profile; when am I going to be paid for what I do? I deserve a full-time position. How can I serve that person when I am more gifted?' Dove sellers and money changers! 'I will bless them with my gift if I believe they deserve it.' Jonah had that problem. He didn't like God's choice of where God had commanded him to use his gift. He was a racist. How many spiritual racists do we have sitting in church? How many refuse to bless people with their God-given gift because of prejudice, offence, unforgiveness or pride?

Finally ...

We can't fool Jesus – he knows our thoughts and intents. He is coming to his temple – our hearts – to overturn our hidden agendas and turf us out of seats we should never sit on and challenge attitudes that restrict his blessing the world. How does he do it? By sending his Word to run wild.

3

The Word Gone Wild

I love the kind of TV programmes that take you behind the scenes to show how things are made, achieved or even completed. I have often been amazed at stunning special effects that recreated lifelike events, whether it be the incredible final scenes in the movie *Titanic* where Jack and Rose are holding on for their lives while poised precariously hundreds of feet up on the rear end of a ship gazing down at what could only be a watery grave, or the scenes from the stunning *Deep Impact* that graphically and realistically recreate a massive tsunami that rises up as a nautical fist ready to smash down on Manhattan.

The question – fuelled by our inquisitive natures – that rises within us is simply, 'How did they do that?' There used to be a very popular children's TV programme called *How?* which sought to answer the questions we sometimes ask concerning things that seem complex, and to show how they work, function and operate – questions such as 'How does snow form?' 'Why do birds migrate?' 'How can a bumblebee fly?'

The amazing picture of Jesus, the living Word, running wildly and violently around the temple driving out the spiritual parasites and prostitutes, is a perfect visual example of what God desires to do in our heart. This incident not only helps us understand why God desires to cleanse our heart but, just as importantly, it shows us how he does it.

Hebrews 4:12 put under the microscope gives us some startling insight into how God uses his living Word to cleanse the temple of our heart and sweep clean a place where he can dwell with pleasure: 'For the word of God is living and powerful, and sharper than any two-edged sword, piercing even to the division of soul and spirit, and of joints and marrow, and is a discerner of the thoughts and intents of the heart.'

That is a wonderful description of what the living Word does. It is God's interrogator, his detergent, his truth serum, his scalpel – whatever he needs to do to bring our heart back into line with what he intended it to be.

Living …

'For the word of God is living': Jesus, the living Word, was not static in the temple that day; no one could contain him. He moved swiftly, purposefully and, to the religious eye, unpredictably. The Word is alive, it is active. And this is what happens when the Word comes off the pages of the Bible and into your heart – it doesn't just sit there, it goes to work confronting, convicting, cleansing and comforting. That is why when we are not living right before God, we stop reading the Bible. Because once the Word is within, its nature is to move, convicting, overturning and challenging.

... *and powerful*

Not only is the Word living, the verse declares it is 'powerful'. We're not dealing with some lightweight here; it took a strong man to overturn tables weighed down with money, merchandise and mutton – yet he 'overturned' them. The Word of God is powerful. It overturns, like a white corpuscle attacking an area of infection in our body; it knows exactly where to go and what to do. Like *The Terminator*, it doesn't stop until the target is reached and eliminated. The Word of God once sent from his mouth does not, the Bible declares, return to him void (Is. 55:11). It will accomplish its purpose like an unstoppable warrior droid in a sci-fi movie; whatever the defence, it just keeps coming. Aren't those kinds of movies scary? Whatever you do to attempt to stop the onslaught of the programmed pursuer, nothing works. The Word of God is God's unstoppable force: it has been programmed to accomplish, 'to complete the mission' for which it has been sent. The power of God's Word is focused and purposed. The programmer is not some demented, power-crazed tyrant, but a loving God who desires only what is best for us. Through the prophet Isaiah, God assures us he means business when his Word is dispatched: '... it shall prosper in the thing for which I sent it' (Is. 55:11).

The Word of God is powerful; its kick overturns. It overturns the tables of pride, selfishness and deceit that we have erected to sell our prohibited wares. The Word moves because it's alive. It overturns because it is powerful and this verse in Hebrews tells us it has a devastating cutting edge; it also pierces.

Cut to the heart

It is 'sharper than any two-edged sword'. Before you experience the comfort of God's Word, you must first learn to accept the cut. Like Zorro's sword skilfully etching out his mark, declaring to all 'I was here', the mark of God's Word to comfort and cut leaves its unmistakable trademark; one that demands a response. To those who receive Zorro as a friend, the mark comforts; to those who reject Zorro as an enemy, the mark repels. When the Word comes to cut we have a choice of two responses: either to accept or to reject, to co-operate or to resist, to embrace as a friend or repel as an enemy.

There are two incidents in the New Testament where God used his skilfully aimed foil to cut. These are found in Acts 2:36,37 (when Peter addresses the crowd) and Acts 7:51–58 (Stephen before the Sanhedrin) and illustrate my point well. Two different groups of people, yet both cut to the heart by the Word. There were, however, two very different responses. One group called '... what shall we do?' while the other group, in contrast, '... cried out with a loud voice, [and] stopped their ears ...' To avoid words they didn't want to hear, like little children, they used their fingers and voices as a preventative measure to defend themselves against the sword of heaven. Have you experienced the cut of the Spirit's samurai sword? Has a festering sore been exposed that needs healing and attention? Or are you continually living in denial, as the pus of a lanced boil of a bad attitude, soiled integrity or illicit relationship runs down your spiritual skin? The Word of God has come to cut; are you raising your voice and stopping your ears to drown out its command so you can continue to rationalise your lifestyle, defend your opinion or blame your circumstances? Take your lead from the other group, the group that cried out for immediate comfort to the exposed infection opened up by the divine surgeon's scalpel. 'What must I do? What needs to change? Who needs to go? What needs to stop?'

For a number of years, we held an annual conference in our church which attracted many hundreds of people. In 1997, my wife of 26 years left the church, our home and me (we divorced in October 1998). As you can imagine the effect on my life and the church's life was devastating. Hundreds of people left the church, my reputation was severely marred and the temptation to give up was a daily battle. In July 1999, while preaching at a church in Oslo, I shared for the first time publicly what it was like as a minister to go through a divorce. In the congregation was a lady called Laila who was going through something similar to what I had shared. We met after one of the sessions and she gratefully thanked me for having the courage to be honest about the failure of my marriage. 'It gives hope for someone sitting in the pew,' she said. It is encouraging to know that even preachers get it wrong sometimes! We both felt a connection and developed a relationship (mainly by telephone) over the next year. In July 2000 we were married at the King's Church in Newport by Laila's pastor from Norway, Pastor Aage Aaleskjaer. My remarriage caused as much of a negative reaction as my divorce.

The lesson I'm leading up to was learned during our 2000 Impact Conference; the speakers had been invited, the conference had been widely advertised and we were ready to roll. I was excited to open the conference on the Wednesday night and walked into the hall ready to preach the opening message. I was expecting, and accustomed to, a packed house. I discovered to my surprise that the hall wasn't even one-third full. I struggled to preach that night, desperately trying to hide my disappointment. I went home and lay next to my wife, as miserable as sin and dreading having to preach at the first session the following morning, fearing no one would come.

'Why are you so quiet?' my wife asked.

'Oh, I'm just depressed because of the attendance tonight. We usually get three times more people attending on our opening night,' I said. 'It's not a good start.'

She turned to me quietly but, speaking deliberately, told me, 'You're not depressed because of the attendance. You're depressed because your pride is hurt. You're depressed because of what others will think.'

I listened with my mouth open, but she didn't let up.

'Who is preaching in the morning?' she asked.

'I am,' I answered sheepishly.

'Well, I'm going to pray that no one turns up. God obviously has to deal with your pride, not your disappointment.'

God used my wife to wield his sword to cut open an undetected infection in my heart. I had not realised how much I had relied on successful conferences, the reputation of one of the fastest growing churches in Wales and the admiration and respect I received as a result. I realised I had become 'addicted to approval'[7] as Joyce Meyer puts it; I had become a success junkie.

The attendance at that conference was not great but the Holy Spirit did a work in my heart, cutting away junk from my motives and released me from a crippling addiction I never realised held me so tight. God used the negative public reaction to my divorce and remarriage to face up to an arrogance and praise-dependency I didn't really know I had. I understood now why Jesus allowed Peter to fail, because after he recovered he would minister with a more merciful heart, humble mind and purer motives. I knew this had been the case for me. I could have lived in denial as the Word came and 'cut [me] to the heart'.

Finally ...

I'm so glad that by God's help I was able to respond with ears unstopped and voice subdued, humbly and reverently asking the heavenly swordsman, 'What must I do?' I know you will too!

4

The Word Gone Deep

If I develop a serious physical problem deep inside my body, by simply visiting a pharmacist I can receive something to relieve the pain. If I visit a nurse she could try her best, using all her expertise, to make me as comfortable as possible; I could even visit my GP who could give a general diagnosis of my condition. But because of the nature and location of the complaint only the surgeon, because he has the trained skill to go deep inside my body, could eradicate the danger.

Dividing soul and spirit ...

Friends can help with pain, family can provide wonderful comfort; pastors and ministers can possibly give you a spiritual diagnosis but no one can do what the Word can do. Like the surgeon, no one else is qualified to go where the Word can go. The Word goes deeper than any pain relief a friend may give, deeper than the comfort of the closest relative and deeper than the wisdom of any human counsellor. As we continue to look at Hebrews 4:12, we can see that this verse describes the penetrative ability of the Word of God to pierce even to the division of soul and spirit, joint and marrow, thoughts and intents. Now *that's* deep!

The Word moves because it's alive; it overturns because it's powerful; it pierces because it's sharp and it divides because it's skilfully selective. Like a wise surgeon, it knows how to divide bad tissue from good tissue. Like an experienced vine dresser, it knows how to divide the unproductive from the fruitful and, just like a skilled chef, it separates the edible from the inedible. It has the amazing ability to divide soul and spirit. As we fill our hearts with God's Word and allow it to do its work, we will become trained and conditioned to live our Christian lives less from our soul and more from our spirits, simply because the Word has the ability to execute such a division. Because of the Word's ability in this area, it helps release us to live our lives energised by our redeemed spirit rather than by the emotional limitations of our soul. We will learn to go from emotion to devotion, from moods to maturity, from feelings to faith. It's time to realise experientially the joy of living with our emotions submitted to our convictions, our feelings submitted to our faith and our passion submitted to our principles. The Word allowed to go deep, dividing soul from spirit, is our only hope of living that way.

Emotional thieves

When the children of Israel stood on the banks of the River Jordan ready to cross over into the Promised Land, it wasn't the presence of giants or the scale of the task or even their lack of experience in warfare that robbed them of God's promised blessing. It was much simpler than that. Their biggest problem was deep within their souls. The same reason they failed to enjoy what God had prepared and promised is the same reason *we* fail to claim and enjoy what he has prepared and promised – feelings! One reason we need to go from emotion to devotion is because feelings will always question truth.

Observing Israel's failure to enter the Promised Land, I noticed four emotional thieves at work (Num. 13:31 – 14:2). Firstly, the feeling of intimidation: 'We are not able to go up against the people . . .' Secondly, we see inferiority eroding confidence like a snowball on a fire: '. . . we were like grasshoppers in our own sight . . .' Fear was close on their heels when they considered the task ahead and the price they had to pay: they '. . . lifted up their voices and cried, and . . . wept that night.' And the ball and chain that really dragged them to the bottom of uselessness was the heavy weight of self-pity: '. . . if only we had died in this wilderness!' they pathetically whinged.

How many times have we allowed our feelings to so dominate our lives? How many times have we left the door of our hearts unlocked, giving access to those things mentioned above? How many days have been wasted, opportunities passed or time lost because we have allowed our feelings to steer the course for our lives? Christianity would be easy if it wasn't for our humanity! The biggest sacrifice we are ever going to make, as we seek to embrace and complete our destiny, is not financial or relational but emotional. Any feeling that refuses to embrace, does not agree with, or does not submit to, the promise of God, is a lie. Any feeling that demands obedience over God's Word is an enemy and should be treated as such. The feeling itself is not a lie, its language is.

Goliath was not a lie, he was real enough. But when he started to verbally undermine and challenge God and his Word, that's when his mouth had to be shut. Our feelings are real enough; we don't live in denial of them, but when fear says 'You can't do it', worry says 'You'll never make it', hatred says 'They deserve it', and bitterness says 'Don't forget it', that's when the language of feelings needs to be silenced.

'But Ray,' I can hear you say, 'that's impossible. That voice is so persistent, so loud and so persuasive. How can I live without that negative influence?'

I'm glad you asked because I'm not talking about denying these feelings, I'm talking about ignoring them.

I was so inspired by the movie *A Beautiful Mind*, where Russell Crowe brilliantly portrayed the life of the troubled genius John Forbes Nash Jnr, a unique mathematician who was awarded the Nobel Prize for his contribution to the world of physics. The downside of his brilliance was his delusions. All his life he was plagued by imaginary personalities. He lived for years in a world of fantasy which appeared to him to be frighteningly real. These people who existed only in the private world of his imagination were so powerful in their persuasive influence, so real in their presence and conversation that they nearly drove him to suicide and the murder of his family. In the final scenes of the movie, as he walks away with the prize of achievement under his arm, now an old man and apparently free from his imaginary tormentors, a friend approaches him with words of congratulation and expresses relief that he was finally free from his private prison. Slowly the camera pans round to show, lurking in the background, sinisterly stalking, as if waiting eagerly to start their 'head games' all over again, the imaginary characters, as real as ever. I remember sitting there waiting for John Forbes's answer to his friend's rush of celebration over his apparent freedom. He simply looked at his emotional stalkers, smiled at his friend and said that they were still there and just as real but he had just chosen to ignore them. There it is – Hollywood comes to our rescue for once with the key to how to go from emotion to devotion. Our feelings will never go away, they are still as real as ever, but by faith, we don't have to listen to their lies any more as they try to question truth and rob us of its promise.

For example, when the Word declares us righteous, feelings will rise up to question its validity. 'That can't be true!' they shout in defiance. You feel far from holy. Religion is based on that lie because it accepts and responds to the deceptive voice of feelings questioning the truth of imparted righteousness received by faith as a gift from God. The mind then rationalises on some method or course of action needed to experience a feeling of worthiness.

The whirlpool of performance

For years, I was trapped in this whirlpool of performance. I felt compelled to set up my own three-ringed religious circus. I jumped through my religious hoops, walked on my religious tightrope, spun my religious plates hoping the audience of heaven would break out in rapturous applause … but instead, I felt the whip of my lying emotions demanding I perform some more.

Philip Yancey, in his liberating book *What's so Amazing about Grace?*,[8] perfectly captures my frustration during that season of spiritual gymnastics. Instead of the sound of appreciative hand claps, I heard the shouts from the stalls hollering 'Sing the song of the Seven Dwarves', but as I began to sing, instead of the familiar Disney wording, the words that came out of my mouth were 'I owe, I owe, to work I have to go', and the leering audience of lying emotion clapped in appreciation some more. And did I work! I increased my Bible reading, church attendance, changed my code of dress and adjusted my tone of voice. I attended every meeting that had the likelihood of increasing my favour with heaven. I became a Pentecostal monk living in my own portable monastery of detachment and drudgery. I totally related to Martin Luther who, like John Forbes Nash, had his own destructive emotional stalkers.

The only way he believed he could enjoy the smile of God was to impress heaven with his spiritual workaholic lifestyle. In his pursuit for holiness, not only did he make the decision to become a Catholic monk, but to be the most intense in his attempt to scale every mountain of spiritual discipline that would eventually prepare him to be fit for heaven. He would sleep fewer hours, he would fast more meals, spend more time in confession ... One day they found him lying on the floor of his room close to death worn out from his religious works and feelings of despair. Raised against a Catholic background of mysticism and religious duty, he was taught that Jesus, Mary and the saints behaved much better than they needed to while on earth and as a result had stored extra credit of holiness in heaven, and that reservoir of extra holiness was available for anyone who worked hard enough or was wealthy enough to pay the price. Those credits of righteousness, he was told, were stored in a heavenly banking system which was monitored by the Pope. Those credits of goodness were available to the common people through assigned activities from the priests, called works, which when performed would then give a receipt called an indulgence. No matter what Luther did, religion demanded more.

Finally, to his rescue came the sabre of salvation, cutting through the career of holiness by performance as it divided soul from spirit. 'The just shall live by faith' (Rom. 1:17). With one skilful swipe of the Master's sword, Luther was free, his soul cleanly divided from his spirit, with his life transformed and the religious world reformed; the discovery that the currency of penance his feelings demanded could be forever ignored, as his spirit embraced the truth of justification by faith.

Finally ...

Start today! Train your feelings to follow your faith; do not put the cart of emotion before the horse of conviction. Direct the power of your passion through the cable of principle and experience the yoke that is easy and the burden that's light.

5

The Word Gone Relational

Every Christmas we have a culinary ritual in our home. It is a wonderful Norwegian tradition, concerning the preparation and presentation of a classic Norwegian dish called 'Pinnekjott' (pronounced 'Pin-e-chert'). The whole process centres on a lamb and, when complete, I have the privilege of eating at the best restaurant in the world – our house! The food is cooked by the most attractive skilled chef I have ever seen – my wife, and the food is eaten by the most appreciative customer on the planet – me!

My wife never ceases to amaze me as she creates magic in the kitchen. Pulling a rabbit out of a hat is nothing compared with what my wife continuously pulls out of the oven! And at Christmas she puts Cinderella's fairy godmother to shame. Turning pumpkins into golden carriages is nothing compared to what she does with the ribcage of a lamb! I cannot even begin to try to describe the explosion of flavour that fills the mouth as the salted lamb, sweet swede and boiled potato hits the taste buds.

I know the ingredients sound nothing special, but when my wife's creativity touches them …!

The whole process begins with the way the lamb is cut. I am always interested to see the butcher's expression as my wife lays out a full colour photograph of the dissected lamb, each part of its anatomy carefully separated and divided into perfectly sectioned pieces, each labelled into its own specified cut. The butcher's face lights up at the prospect of putting his butchery skills to the test and, with knives sharpened and ready, he masterfully and deliberately cuts and divides bone from flesh and joint from socket until every part is separated according to the pattern presented to him in the picture.

Dividing joint from marrow

What has all this to do with the subject at hand? Well, the verse in Hebrews we have been looking at – 4:12 – uses a very strange term to describe the dividing ability of the Word. It is almost akin to the art of butchery: '… the word of God … piercing even to the division of soul and spirit, and of joints and marrow …' As I watch the butcher carefully divide and separate each bone, rib section, shoulder and leg, I begin to understand what the Holy Spirit shows me. The process of the Word dividing joint from marrow takes on a new fascination, one to investigate!

In our culture, this is a difficult phrase to understand but to the Jewish mind it was simple. The phrase was commonly used to determine the selection, segregation and division concerning relationships. The Hebrews talked about 'live bone' and 'dead bone'. The live bone is the marrow-filled blood cell factory producing life for the body. The dead bone produces nothing; it contributes no vital ingredients to keep the body alive, it is merely structural. The Bible has a lot to say about relationships, the development of them and the division of them. The Word of God talks about relationships that are productive – 'marrow', and those that are not – 'joints'. If ever there was a time we needed to rely on its ability to help us discern between the two, it is today. Sometimes there will be a conflict of interest between joint and marrow, dead bone and live bone or a conflict between unproductive, unhealthy relationships and those divinely orchestrated relationships, full of marrow, full of productivity, full of life. These are the relationships that build you up, fuelling your propulsion as you reach for your God-given destiny. The Word has the ability to give you wisdom to help you divide one from the other so you can make a choice which influence to follow.

Recently, I conducted a nine-week series of teaching in my church called 'Burying the Lies about Singleness'.[9] In the process of raising three teenage children, and observing as a pastor the emotional casualties on the killing fields of dating amongst the singles in our church, a growing passion developed out of a real desire to help them steer their way through this devastating minefield. The response to the series was amazing. Single people of all ages – teenagers, young adults, widows, widowers, older unmarried and divorcees – were so encouraged that I knew I had to get the material into book-form to help a wider audience.

One of the surprises to me was the response from parents with teenage children. 'Thank you, Pastor!' was the response from many parents who were at their wits' end as to how to counsel their children concerning boyfriends, girlfriends, courting and dating. 'This has really helped us to help our children through a war zone!'

The response from others was, 'I wish someone taught me this stuff when I was young.' One man in his early twenties said, 'Pastor, it's not just a minefield out there, it's an emotional Vietnam.' I didn't really understand just what single people have to face, until at fifty years of age, I found myself single. Speaking the Word of God to 30,000 people was easy compared to the dating game. My wife Laila and I have now been married for five and a half years, at the time of writing; it's a miracle we're together. If it had been down to my dating skills, I'd still be single! But through personal interaction with my stepchildren, observation, and compassion for the singles in my own church (as well as the scary experience of my own journey) I have felt compelled to explore what the Word had to say in the whole area of romantic relationships, and see how we can rely upon the Word to help us divide joint from marrow – productive relationships from non-productive.

We throw our arms up in horror as we gaze at the casualties caused by recent natural disasters, such as over 200,000 killed by the Indian Ocean tsunami, a city in America totally eradicated by Hurricane Katrina, and approximately 50,000 crushed by an earthquake in Northern India, many of them children. We are stunned by images of twisted, bloodied, dismembered bodies caused by the attack of terrorists and international war. We send millions of pounds as an outward indication of how we feel their pain and desire to help. But we ignore the scale of devastation in our schools, churches and families caused by the misuse, breakdown and ignorance concerning relationships. 'A little over the top, Ray! Don't you think you're being a little dramatic? It's good and normal for teenagers to experiment a little with dating multiple partners! Surely they gain experience for the future?' Tell that to those who have to raise children when they want to experience the joy of childhood themselves. Tell that to those who daily live with the guilt of having aborted a life they feel they could not bring into the world. Tell that to three teenage Norwegian boys who, unknown to each other, in three separate incidents, committed suicide because their girlfriends broke up with them. Talk to the girl ravaged by rape while trusting her boyfriend because he told her he loved her. Talk to the 50,000 or so teenage girls who every year are told they have Chlamydia, a sexually transmitted disease which has stolen their rights to be mothers. Still over the top? I don't think so!

The Bible says we perish because of limited understanding (see Hos. 4:6), and if ever we needed the cutting edge of God's Word to help us discern from live bone and dead bone, joint and marrow, good relationships and bad relationships, it is now. A famous actress encapsulated the philosophy of our culture when she foolishly declared that a woman is desperate to be loved and until she finds it, must experience many relationships. That's the voice of the culture of the world but it is not the voice of God's kingdom. In the area of dating and people experimenting in short-term multiple romantic relationships, we have failed to take note of the casualties, and failed to point people to relationships as God intended.

I recently read this unauthenticated account of something that *could* have happened.[10] Imagine if it had been true! During the Great War, a parachute was invented that was guaranteed 100 per cent safe. It always opened, whoever used it, whatever the size of the person and whatever the circumstance. In order for that percentage of safety to be ensured, meticulous attention had to be given to the way the parachute was folded, for that was the secret of its safety. Every part of the parachute had to be carefully and painstakingly placed in certain positions, which had to follow the manufacturer's instructions. During the war a group of young men, who came to be known as the 'fast folders', influenced the workforce to bypass the manufacturer's process in order to increase productivity. They encouraged the workforce to completely ignore the instruction book, and then introduced a new and faster method. Production increased and everyone was happy – until it became obvious something was radically wrong. They discovered that out of every ten who jumped using the parachute packed by the 'fast folders', nine fell to their deaths. Reports went back to the 'fast folders'; the news of the tragedies broke their hearts, and as a result they immediately returned to the manufacturer's original guide. Others amazingly ignored the facts for which they were responsible, and instead pointed to the few who survived as justification for the new method.

Our church, family and friendship circles are filled with tragic stories of relational deaths; millions are jumping into relationships without correctly folded parachutes. The responsibility for the carnage lies firmly at the feet of the 'fast folders'.

The Passion Fast Folders

We give in to instant gratification as our uncontrolled, undisciplined, insatiable desires cry out, 'It feels good, so why not?' For those reading these words who are blinded by hormonal deceivers that dilute the effects of unbiblical sex, for those who are practising pre-marital or extra-marital sex involving another person *or* pornography – you're jumping to your death with a parachute fast-folded by passion. Our instructor's manual, the Bible, the Word of God, tells us for our own safety, concerning unbiblical sex, run from it (2 Tim. 2:22), kill it (Col. 3:5), stop it (Eph. 5:3–8), expose it (Eph. 5:10–14), expel it (1 Cor. 5:1–5) and disassociate yourself from it (1 Cor. 5:9–12).

The Pulpit Fast Folders

These are preachers who are afraid to hit the issue head on because they don't want to offend. They are empowered by the culture, they want to be liked, or they don't want to make people feel bad. Our mandate as servants of God is the same as Paul gave to his young protégé to preach the Word faithfully whatever the cultural climate, whatever the public reaction and whatever the personal rejection. Many lives are at stake and our responsibility not to fast-fold God's principles concerning unbiblical sex must be a priority.

The Peer Fast Folders

These are other people, maybe friends, who have jumped with fast-folded parachutes and messed their own lives up, but instead of repenting and warning others of the pain of their bad decisions, they seduce whoever they can to do the same, believing 'If others join me, I won't look or feel so bad.'

Parental Fast Folders

Parental Fast Folders are irresponsible parents, too afraid or lazy to give clear boundaries concerning romantic relationships. They are fast-folding their children's parachute and, even worse, standing by and doing nothing as they observe them about to jump into a disastrous relationship situation.

Finally ...

We have all been guilty of fast folding in the area of relationships. Thank God for his forgiveness to the repentant heart, his power to the restored spirit and his wisdom to the teachable mind. He enables us to get up, get over it and start again as he allows the Word to work within us. That Word divides joint from marrow, live bone from dead bone ... and productive relationships from destructive ones.

6

The Word Mending Your Mind

'I don't believe in it, it's a load of rubbish!'
My brother's words hung in the air just waiting to be challenged.

The setting for this outburst and subsequent events was a cabaret club in Wales where I was performing with my band, Robbie Ray and The Jaguars. My brother's remarks were a response to the confident claim of the well-known hypnotist we were supporting. The hypnotist had said that he could control the mind of the most sceptical person in the audience. So my brother, Roland, took it upon himself to accept responsibility for that role.

Egged on by the verbal orchestra playing that soul-stirring symphony 'I dare you', he rose from his seat and strode towards the stage as we chanted 'Go on, son!', 'Go show him, Roland!', 'You're the man!' Of course our ego-energising words did not have an authentic ring to them, because in reality we were hoping the hypnotist was as good as he claimed to be and would reduce Roland to a puppet on a string.

We were not to be disappointed; he was the first and easiest to be put under. We laughed until our sides ached as we saw him being mentally manipulated to simulate a play session with his mates as a three-year-old. The antics had to stop when my brother picked up his imaginary train and began hitting the guy next to him over the head with it! Before the hypnotist released him from his excursion into the past, he gave him a command: 'When you hear me mention the word "Saturday", wherever you are, I want you to stand to your feet and shout at the top of your voice, "Three cheers for the hypnotist!"' He slowly counted back from ten to one and my brother was back to what appeared to be normal. A little dazed and wondering what had happened, he returned to his seat alongside the rest of us, still bragging about how he had beat the performer's powers. As the mind-bender came to the close of his act, he simply said, 'Thank you very much, ladies and gentlemen. I will see you again next Saturday.' Like a programmed robot, my brother stood to his feet, jumped up on the table and in front of all the people made a fool of himself by encouraging all present to shout three cheers for the greatest cabaret act in the world. It was one of the funniest things I'd ever seen.

Since becoming a Christian, I've realised that our minds are very precious – and very vulnerable. The mind should be guarded and, for its own protection, be totally surrendered to the love of God in worship and service. The Word declares that we should love the Lord God with all our heart, soul, strength and mind. The Uri Gellars and David Blaines may be able to impress us with their powers of suggestion, telepathy and thought control, but there is only one thing that can divide thoughts and intents, mind and motive and that is the Word of God. In our fallen world, through gurus, psychics and manipulators, we are encouraged to bend our minds, lend our minds or send our minds. But the Bible exhortation is to mend our minds, in order that we might think clearly, sifting the mental junk that would interfere with us making the right decisions concerning the will of God. Romans 12:2 says '... do not be conformed to this world, but be transformed by the renewing of your mind, that you may prove what is that good and acceptable and perfect will of God.'

God's Word has the amazing ability to divide the thoughts and the intents of our heart. Knowing this truth and living in the power of it is absolutely essential in our warfare with Satan. Most of our warfare with the enemy is conducted in the battlefield of our mind, in our thought life. Realising that not every thought you have is from God, not every thought you have is from the devil, and not every thought you have is from yourself helps tremendously in winning the war against our foe, and brings us into a freedom we've always longed to experience.

The Word of God, the sword of the Spirit, is the way to help you discern the source and origin of our thoughts. Do you realise how powerful that is? Understanding this will change your life.

Jesus demonstrated this in his skirmish with Satan in the wilderness. In the record of this event (Lk. 4:1–13) we see that during all three areas of attacks, Jesus blocked the devil's attempt to distract him by using the sword. 'It is written ...' He was able by using the Word to discern between conviction and condemnation. 'If You are the Son of God ...' was a clever attempt by Satan to sow doubt on Jesus' personal relationship with his Father. Jesus, knowing his Father would never play 'head games' with him in the area of relationship, immediately used the sword to divide thought and intent: 'This is not my thought; I love my Father. This is not from my Father because he loves me. This thought has to come from Satan to sow condemnation and doubt into my life concerning my personal relationship with my Father.' Jesus located the source of the thought and dealt with it accordingly. How many people are living with a source of duty and obligation to perform and please God because they don't know how to differentiate between conviction and condemnation?

The Word was used by Jesus to discern between flesh and spirit. 'If you are, then,' continued Satan, 'prove it! Command these stones to be made bread.' Jesus immediately discerned the fingerprints of Satan all over the suggestion; he knew he didn't have to prove his spirituality or divine favour through performance, power or possessions: 'That thought is directed to my flesh, not my spirit. I don't get my value from my works but his Word. Man shall not live by bread alone but by every word of God.'

From this battle in the wilderness we also learn that the Word will help us discern what is deception and what is divine. 'I will give you the kingdoms of the world if you will just worship me.' Without hesitation, fuelled with the Word, Jesus wielded the sword one more time, slicing the fat of deception from the food of divinity. Isolating the thought aimed at his capacity for pride, he declared, 'Get behind me, Satan! For it is written, "You shall worship the LORD your God, and Him only you shall serve." My destiny is a cross not a career. My mandate is to humble myself, not exalt myself.' And so ended that particular ambush; Satan slunk away, realising what worked on the first Adam failed on the second. It is so important to realise our Father sends his Word to run wild in our lives to perfect us, purify us and protect us.

It is also vital that I explain to you just how God has designed various ways for his Word to gain entrance into our lives. As far as I can see there are five.

The preached Word

The Early Church had a healthy respect for the preached Word, so much so that Acts 2:41,42 tells us that they devoted themselves to it. Devotion to the preached Word is far more than sitting in church on a Sunday morning and listening to the preacher for 45 minutes! When they fulfil their responsibility as the preacher it is then that ours as learners begin. For the preached Word to have full effect in our lives there needs to be three ingredients. The first of these is analysis: 'What is God saying?' The second is accountability: 'What is God saying to me?' And the third is action: 'What is God asking me to do?' God has not placed preachers and teachers in the church for entertainment or as objects for adoration, but to communicate his Word through their mouths in order to effect change. Scriptures such as Luke 8:21, John 13:17, John 15:14 and James 1:22 show that God is not impressed with what you know, but with what you *do* with what you know.

The personal word

The second way God's Word finds entrance into our lives is through the personal word. Whatever your private personal reading plan, it is vital that you sit down with the Holy Spirit, opened Bible before your eyes, and ask him to speak to you. I am amazed how the Holy Spirit on so many occasions has invaded my life with wisdom, comfort and instruction through a 'designer label' personal word; a word to fit my circumstance, with my name written all over it. Maybe a passage of Scripture, or a story you've read many times before suddenly becomes a lifeline to pull you through a stormy season.

It's good to buy a suit off the peg that generally fits you but there is a great difference when you have one tailor-made. That's the difference between the *logos* – the general Word of God, and the *rhema* – the personal word from God. The *logos* is the general revelation of God we all need to hear regularly, but the *rhema*, the personal word, is tailored to our present need.

I remember the pain, shame and grief I experienced while having to deal with a failed marriage. For many weeks, I was unable to preach. Not only had the desire gone but also the ability. I knew the Scriptures, I could remember all the stories, but they were merely informative not medicinal. They were 'suits off the peg', when I needed a perfect fit. Then one day, while playing a round of golf, everything changed. I wasn't feeling particularly spiritual; in fact, I felt my whole emotional structure had been anaesthetised. I was about to take a shot onto the green, when out of the blue the word I needed came. In a flash before my spiritual eyes I saw the story of how the prophet Samuel mourned over the judgement of King Saul. Saul had been placed in a position by God but failed to carry out his heavenly mandate; he became an embarrassment to God, the nation of Israel and also to the prophet Samuel. Even so, Samuel still loved him and mourned deeply over his rejection. While he was still heartbroken over the loss, the word of the Lord came to him and thundered, 'How long will you mourn for Saul, seeing I have rejected him from reigning over Israel? Fill your horn with oil and go; I am sending you to Jesse the Bethlehemite. For I have provided Myself a king among his sons' (1 Sam. 16:1).

I had read that scripture many times but suddenly it became personal. For many weeks I had been mourning over the breakdown of my marriage, immobilised by grief and condemnation. His Word came to me as it did to Samuel, 'Stop mourning what I've judged! It's time to move on; there is a destiny to complete.' I can't begin to tell you how instantly releasing that moment was. God had sent his word, tailor-made; it fitted. It felt good, and from that moment on I began my recovery.

Never forget, God has a personal word to guide you through the seasons of life. Expect these words. Receive them. Use them.

The prophesied word

When I speak of the prophesied word, I am not talking about some flaky ambiguous inference by some self-styled prophet who believes their verbal rubbish becomes sanctified because of the final: 'Thus says the Lord!' I'm talking about those words spoken over you that find a resting place in your heart. In the same way that Mary, the mother of Jesus, pondered over words spoken concerning her son and her destiny, there are morsels of divine substance lying dormant in your soul awaiting an appropriate time to be regurgitated, remembered and rejoiced over.

The events at Jerusalem after Jesus was crucified had sent shock waves through the lives of his followers; they were devastated, fearful, angry and very vulnerable. Out of all his followers, the women were the only ones to rise above the black clouds of negativity and hopelessness. Why? Luke 24:8 tells us it was because '... they remembered His words'.

'He is not here, but is risen! Remember how He spoke to you ... in Galilee' (Lk. 24:6). The angel was encouraging them to remember how Jesus had explained the events prior to his crucifixion and resurrection: 'Well, ladies, he meant what he said.' They remembered his words and were lifted above the storm of doubt, depression and fear and began to fly in clear skies.

It's time to remember those words Jesus spoke to you through personal prophecy. You wondered at the time what they meant; they didn't fit your (then) circumstance, but now they do. We easily forget God sees into our tomorrows; not only is he acquainted with our present needs but our future ones and he makes provision to face and overcome them before we arrive.

So, the prophesied word – it's time to remember his words to 'Fear not' when you weren't afraid; remember his comforting words 'I am with you always' when you felt his presence so close; and remember the time he said 'You shall not want' when you lacked for nothing. Maybe some reading these words need to remember the revelation he gave that 'There is . . . now no condemnation' when you didn't feel like a failure. It's time to remember those words brought to you on the wings of prophesy that 'all things work together for good', given when your world was in no need of repair. God's answer for you during seasons of doubt, discouragement or despair can very often be closer than you think, in the prophesied word remembered!

Paul's advice to Timothy when experiencing seasons of satanic onslaught was, remember the personal prophesied word and use it as a weapon: 'This charge I commit to you, son Timothy, according to the prophecies made concerning you, that by them you may wage the good warfare' (1 Tim. 1:18).

The personified Word

Fourthly, God uses the Word made flesh, Bibles with legs, epistles with skin. Never be intimidated or angry when observing the challenging qualities of another person's life. God is using them, his personified Word, to overturn some tables in your life, exposing the hardness in your own heart. So, when someone refuses to laugh at your dirty joke, when someone refuses to lose their temper and remains calm when you want revenge, or when someone refuses to nurture their hurt with words such as 'How could they?' when you continue to nurse and rehearse yours, don't be irritated by their behaviour. Thank God! He is using them as his personified Word to challenge you and bring about change in your life.

The proclaimed word

Finally, there is the proclaimed word. You do not want to be on the receiving end of this one! When it comes there is no negotiation, no bargaining and no reasoning. It is declared and it is unchangeable. It is the end of God's patience. It is when God says, 'Enough is enough!' It is the word that sent Ananias and Sapphira to an early grave (see Acts 5:1–10). It is the word that caused Elymas the sorcerer to learn brail for a time (Acts 13:8–11). It's the word that emptied the house of Pharoah of the laughter of his firstborn.

Finally …

Today if you hear his voice, whichever way it comes, harden not your heart. You're going to need it to divide the thought and intents that could so easily shipwreck your faith if not censored by God's Word.

7

A Pure Heart

I once read a story[11] about a Russian school-teacher who
stood up before her class and proudly declared, 'One
of our astronauts, Yuri Gagarin, has successfully left the
earth's atmosphere and orbited the earth.' The class cheered
in shared patriotism. The teacher continued, desiring to
marinate their minds with Soviet atheism. 'And while he
was there, he looked for God but all he saw was space and
stars. So you see, children, it proves what we teach is true.
God does not exist.'

One little girl with a basic knowledge of the Scriptures
put up her hand and said, 'Miss, I think I know why Yuri
Gagarin didn't see God.'

'Why is that?' replied the teacher condescendingly.

'Because he didn't have a pure heart, Miss; the Bible
says, Miss, "Blessed are the pure in heart, for they shall
see God."'

There are a number of reasons why purity of heart
is essential in the Christian life but the pivotal one is
connected with our relationship with, and revelation of,

God. Jesus said it is only the pure in heart that can relate to and see God. The word 'see' in the Greek language means 'to gaze with wide-open eyes at something remarkable'. The look on Elliot's face as he encounters ET for the first time says it all. Have we lost that sense of wonder in our relationship with God? Has our relationship with God been reduced to a casual glance, a 'take it or leave it' observance from a distance? Jesus wants us to 'see', to gaze with wide-open eyes at something remarkable. Purity is the key to such a privilege.

God is pure. His eyes are pure, his ways are pure (Ps. 145:17) and his words are pure (Ps. 12:6). The commandments of the Lord are pure and his home is pure (Rev. 21:27) and so it is only natural that his children should be pure – see Hebrews 12:14, Psalm 24:3,4.

Thank God, that because of the new birth we have been given pure hearts as a free gift (Eph. 2:8,9), but along with that wonderful gift comes a sobering responsibility. Right through the New Testament, there is a continual plea for us to co-operate with God to maintain that purity. The incentive for me to keep pure is not the fear of losing my salvation but the revelation of the wonder of it: '… everyone,' John says, 'who has this hope in Him purifies himself, just as He is pure' (1 Jn. 3:3).

You may have a brand new battery in your car but the key to releasing its power is the purity of the contacts. If the contacts are allowed to become corroded or dirty, the potential power is prevented from being received. It is the same with our brand new heart. It has everything we need to communicate with God but life has a way of corroding the contacts. God has done his part; now we must co-operate with him to keep the contacts clean. Paul's command to Timothy is also a directive for us, '… keep yourself pure' (1 Tim. 5:22), as is his exhortation to the Hebrew Christians, 'Make every effort to live in peace with all men and to be holy; without holiness no-one will see the Lord' (Heb. 12:14, NIV).

There are many other reasons why purity is a must. Purity is essential for effective witness. We have been commissioned to shine as lights in a dark world. The reason a lighthouse can send out its warning beam miles across the raging sea is because of the relationship between the source of light and the reflectors. Surrounding the massive light bulb are hundreds of little mirrors. They are close together so the light can be more concentrated. They are pliable so they can be used in any direction. But they have to be clean, they have to be free from any dirt, dust or grime, otherwise the light will be wasted.

We are not the source of light. Jesus is! But we are made in his image. In other words, we are his reflectors. We are called to be reflectors . . . not absorbers. Max Lucado, in his book *It's Not About Me*,[12] uses the metaphor of the sun's relationship with the moon. The moon works together with the sun. The moon generates no light apart from the sun. The moon is nothing more than a pitch black piece of rock, but properly positioned, the moon beams. Let the cow jump over it, astronauts walk on it, it never objects. Even though sunning is accepted and mooning is not, the moon is at peace, working together with the sun to throw its soft light onto the earth.

We are designed to reflect God's glory, not absorb it; to reflect his light, not retain it. What a wonderfully freeing revelation to realise that both globally and personally, the world doesn't revolve around us! The catastrophic disaster caused by the devastating tsunami in the Indian Ocean on Boxing Day 2004 demonstrated the incredible generosity and compassion resident in the human heart. The amazing compassion of people directed practically toward helping those devastated countries ripped apart by that unprecedented tidal wave demonstrated the wonderful potential to beat this ravaging disease 'It's all about me'. There were incredible acts of heroism, breathtaking scenes of personal sacrifice; unbelievable amounts of compassion oozed from human beings all around the world. Our nation looked away from itself to ease the pain of others. You don't complain of having no shoes when you see someone who has no feet.

Purity of heart is also essential in our warfare with the devil. In this context, Jesus said 'the ruler of this world [Satan] is coming, and he has nothing in Me' (Jn. 14:30) – in other words, 'The devil has scrutinised my life to see if there is any place he can legally reside and he has found none.' Paul's instruction to Timothy to keep his heart pure was a military term. My home country of Wales has hundreds of castles and not far from my home there is such a castle, one with a long history of battles; battles both won and lost. When these castles were built, great pains were taken to ensure they were well fortified. Surrounding the castle as the first line of defence was a deep trench filled with water known as the 'moat'. The second line of defence was the thick, high walls built to accommodate many fighting men. These men were armed with arrows, and boiling oil which they rained down on their enemy as their foe attempted to break the defence. In the event that the moat and walls were breached, all the valuables were collected and taken to an inner castle even more fortified. This inner castle was called a 'keep'.

This is the thought Paul had in mind concerning the precious valuable called 'purity': 'Keep the purity of your heart as a military general would guard that which was most precious when under attack.' Satan is not only after your peace, joy and health; he's after your purity. Why? Because a Christian with a pure heart, according to Jesus, is 'blessed'. He knows your 'blessedness' is connected with your relationship and your relationship is connected with your purity; and your purity is connected with your heart. He goes for the centre of operations. He wants to corrode the contacts. When the Bible talks about our hearts, it refers to the centre of our being, the seat of our affections, imaginations, morality, reasoning powers, perception, conscience, intentions, motives and emotions. Satan is always trying to disrupt communications between you and God by going for the heart. He is going after the 'inner you' where motives are formed, decisions are made, where conscience patrols and imaginations are painted.

Using this method Satan was able to pollute and divide even Jesus' team. John 13:2 tells us that '... supper being ended, the devil having already put it *into the heart* of Judas Iscariot ... to betray Him' (my italics). Satan had entered the keep. The way in was through Judas' greed. No moat had to be negotiated, no towering walls needed to be breached; through Judas' selfishness, he himself lowered the drawbridge and laid out the welcome mat inviting the enemy to take what he wanted. For three years, Satan observed Judas' double life. He was a pretend disciple, a double agent. While he looked good on the outside, he could not resist the temptation to steal from the funds, for which he was responsible, that were used to support the team (see Jn. 12:6).

Satan tried the same method to pollute the Early Church, but strong disciplined leadership shut the door in his face. In Acts 5 we read that Ananias and Sapphira wanted the credibility of discipleship without the integrity needed to earn it. Everyone was sacrificially giving to meet a need in the lives of others. Some even sold houses and Ananias and Sapphira also sold possessions but, pretending to give everything, kept back part of the money for themselves. The source of hypocrisy was targeted when Peter, under the guidance of the Holy Spirit, said, 'Ananias, why has Satan filled your heart to lie to the Holy Spirit and keep back part of the price of the land for yourself?' (v. 3) Satan lost this time. Ananias and Sapphira dropped dead in the sight of all observing and the pollution was stopped.

We must constantly place that which we hold valuable concerning our relationship with God in the keep, especially our purity. If not, we lower the drawbridge and give Satan access to pollute our conscience, morality, imagination, affections, perception and motives.

A deeper understanding of the word 'pure' will help us to be more specific in our defences. The English language compared to the Greek used in the New Testament is very limited in its expression and so it is with the word 'pure'. This word was used in ancient Eastern culture in four ways.

Clothes washed clean

Firstly, it was used to describe soiled clothes washed clean. Using the word in this context, a pure heart is a clean heart. Satan's desire to 'soil' the heart is usually attempted through the 'eye gate'. We are living in a video, movie, and Internet generation. Everything is visual. The stimulation of sexual lust through the 'eye gate' has never been as rampant as it is today. We now have a new type of addict – the sex addict, and one of the main doorways into this addiction is video and Internet pornography. The temptation to commit sexual immorality in the heart has never been as powerful as it is in this generation.

Jesus said in Matthew 5:27,28, 'You have heard that it was said, "Do not commit adultery." But I tell you that anyone who looks at a woman lustfully has already committed adultery with her in his heart' (NIV). There are many, particularly young men, who will read these words and get paranoid because they have been attracted by a good-looking girl. In Jesus' day there were a group of Pharisees who were referred to as the 'Bruised and Bleeding Pharisees'. They believed that it was evil even to look at a woman. So whenever they saw a woman approaching they would close their eyes and keep walking. On many occasions they would walk straight into a wall or fall into a ditch and injure themselves. It sounds funny, I know, but there are many young men beating themselves up believing they have committed adultery in their hearts because they have found a young lady attractive.

If you are one of those young men, let me help you to stop walking into walls. The word Jesus used here – 'lustfully' – is a strong word and has premeditated inference to it. The word means to look with the intention to arouse sexual desire – a *deliberate* use of the eyes to awaken sexual desire.

Here is a practical scenario. You browse through the TV guide and notice there is a programme airing at a certain time with strong sexual content. All day long the thought is circling in your mind of what might be shown in this programme. You arrive home and at the stated time you switch on the TV, sit down and watch, knowing full well you will be sexually aroused. I would class that as committing adultery in the heart – not a casual look at an attractive woman. Let's guard our 'eye gate' and protect our hormones from running wild.

Winnowed and sifted

A second use of the word 'pure' is when corn is winnowed and sifted, purified of chaff. We have to continually work with God as he desires to search and sift our hearts of impurity in our motives. David, realising the need for this cardio-winnowing because of the heart's deceptive potential, cried to God: 'Search me, O God, and know my heart; Try me, and know my anxieties; And see if there is any wicked way in me, And lead me in the way everlasting' (Ps. 139:23,24).

As I've got older I've come to realise that success is not *what* you've accomplished but *why* you've accomplished. We will not be judged for quantity but quality. The Bible says that the *quality* of a person's work will be tested (see 1 Cor. 3:13). People see the outside; God sees the heart. People focus on the fruit of success; God focuses on the root. The recipient of the greatest compliment that Jesus paid to an individual was Nathanael; Nathanael was not commended for his gifting, his intellect or his hard work, or even his social standing. The medal of honour was placed on his heart. 'Jesus saw Nathanael coming toward Him, and said of him, "Behold, an Israelite indeed, in whom there is no deceit!"' (Jn. 1:47). What a compliment! If Jesus were to pay me any compliment, I pray it would be that one: 'Behold a man in whom motives are pure.'

An army purged

The third use of this word 'pure' in biblical times was to describe an army purged of discontented, cowardly, unwilling and inefficient people. Applied to our hearts it would mean a heart that is single. That is, a heart that is individual; a heart with no trace of treason. A heart that understands this world is not our home.

One of the saddest incidents in the New Testament concerns a man called Demas, a close co-worker with the apostle Paul. Paul writes to his spiritual son Timothy with a heavy heart over the departure of this trusted and loved fellow labourer. His disappointment is captured in nine words '... Demas has forsaken me, having loved this present world' (2 Tim. 4:10) – 'He has forsaken me not because of persecution or embarrassment or the challenge of commitment, but because of a choice to fall out of love with his Saviour and into love with his temporal world.' His heart was up for grabs and the world took it. What a sobering lesson for us all to keep our heart pure in its affections, and purged of treason.

Watered down

The fourth use of 'pure' was to describe the process in which milk or wine is watered down or where a metal has been processed until there is no tinge of alloy left. A pure heart is an uncompromising heart. Irrespective of the company we are in, we do not water down our witness to correspond with the social temperature. In this regard many are like Pilate, who, when faced with an opportunity to declare his belief in the Son of God, washed his hands in an attempt to avoid the personal responsibility of aligning himself with Christ. Some fear, like Pilate, that they will lose popularity with the crowd or favour with their peers.

Finally ...

Left to our own devices, the task of walking with a pure heart in this impure and imperfect world would be like hacking our way through the dense jungle of the Amazon with a penknife. To maintain a clean heart, God has provided us with light to keep our thoughts pure. To maintain a sifted heart he has showered his love into our hearts in massive doses so we can reject and resist the cancer of polluted motives (see 1 Jn. 5:2). When the world dangles its lures in front of us, baiting us, tempting us, desiring to hook us and pull us away from our pure devotion to Christ, our faith rises up and turns the other way so we can say with the apostle John: '... this is the victory that has overcome the world – our faith' (1 Jn. 5:4;

see also 1 Jn. 1:7). We should thank God for faith – the key to keeping our heart focused.

The name of Jesus is our weapon when the enemy tries to dilute our passion to stand up and be counted. To run our race with an uncompromising heart, a heart that is fixed steady, true and pure, we respond with the revelation from heaven: '... whoever confesses Me before men, him will I also confess before My Father who is in heaven' (Mt. 10:32).

Ask the Holy Spirit to continually work in you creating a clean heart, a pure heart, a heart that is able to gaze with wide-open eyes at something remarkable. 'Blessed are the pure in heart, For they shall see God' (Mt. 5:8).

8

The Marinated Heart

While deep in thought and meditating over a particular message I was preparing, a sentence paraded itself on the stage of my mind. It shouted, 'Marinate the church!' I immediately recognised the voice of the Holy Spirit but could not understand the implication of the command. I felt a little like Peter after receiving a vision on the rooftop of a house (see Acts 10); willing to obey, but not understanding how.

As I sat quietly, in the theatre of my heart, the Holy Spirit began to explain to me from the stage of my spirit just exactly what he meant: 'I long for the world to taste and see that I am good; I desire to do it through my church, but she has become inedible and tasteless. I'm calling my ministry gifts to marinate so she can become the vehicle to deliver the food.'

Then I remembered the words of Jesus to his disciples when perhaps up to 20,000 hungry people were looking to have their hunger satisfied. As the disciples came to Jesus, believing they were making him aware of the problem, he simply said, 'You give them something to eat' (Mt. 14:16b). There it is. The world is starving for the goodness of God. We have to become edible in order for that need to be met. Jesus is the Bread of Life; he fed the multitudes 2,000 years ago not only physically but spiritually, mentally and emotionally. He still desires to do that today through his body on earth – the church.

Get marinated!

It's time to get marinated, to be tasty … edible! As Jesus was in the world, so are we. Sinners flocked to him; they were attracted to him. They came in their thousands. He was known as a friend of sinners. They ate up his words, they savoured the aroma of his presence and they were sustained, energised and satisfied with the luscious fruit of his life; the fruit of joy, healing and love. He was tasty. He was edible. The people tasted and experienced the goodness of God through the person of Jesus Christ.

Could it be the reason why our churches are not filled is the result not of a disinterested world but of a tasteless church? For me, once you have tasted lamb marinated in mint you are no longer attracted to lamb cooked with no flavour. The answer to a hungry world is not an evangelising church but a marinated one. Offering people tasteless food may satisfy our conscience but it will never satisfy the spiritual taste buds of the lost. The lack of success in our winning the world to Christ is not presentation but marination. We can arrange programmes, events, camps and Bible studies; we can use all the correct scriptures explaining salvation. But unless our lives are marinated with divine spices it is like offering a person unprepared meat – they just don't want it. God is instructing his ministry gifts all over the world to marinate the church so the world may taste and see that he is a good God.

We need to be marinated with mercy not judgement. In *The Power of One Christ-like Life*, Francis Frangipane categorises people into three groups, the largest being the people who peruse the world's sin and corruption, considering change impossible. They feel unable to cope and so retreat into a 'shelter of apathy', cutting themselves off from the world that God wants to reach; in doing so, they become a navel-gazing religious cult.

The second group are totally opposite to the first group. They rail at the storm of evil rather than run from it. He writes:

> They rage at the depravity of the Godly and protest the audacity of the wicked. They pound pulpits and sidewalks. They are both vocal and visible. Yet their ability to affect positive societal change has been for the most part neutralised by their negativity and rage. Sinners cannot endure the harshness of their approach. The problem is they are troubled that the world is un-Christian without being troubled that their hearts are un-Christ like.

The third group is what I believe to be the emerging church that will meet the need the way God intends. Francis Frangipane writes that this group, without minimising the reality and effects of sin, understand that the goal is to win our war not just react to the battle. They understand that the objective of God goes beyond the elimination of evil. They understand God does not seek revenge but redemption. They understand God will not release his divine wrath until he fully exhausts his divine mercy. Our goal is not just the exposure of sin; it is also the unveiling of the sacrifice for sin. This group understand they are maximising mercy, not minimising sin, for there's a difference between *white-washing* and *blood-washing* sin. For too long the world has seen the church about to throw rocks. For too long the Church has been focusing on what's *wrong* with the world, spending its time exposing it. But Jesus Christ saw what was wrong – and died for it. Christians who are judgemental justify their anger at a Godless society by calling it 'righteous indignation'. But they totally miss the point. The thing that angered Jesus was the lack of love and the lack of intercession in his people, not the sin in society. The Bible says that mercy triumphs over judgement. An angry church is useless at dispensing God's mercy because it is consumed with retribution, judgement and revenge.[13]

The source of our motive in reaching out to this world is not revenge but redemption, not dispensing wrath with a closed fist but the offer of reconciliation with an open hand, and Jesus died to show he is serious about it. Jesus did not die with a pointing finger but with outstretched arms. The church needs to put its sword of judgement away and hold out a healing hand.

In the Garden of Gethsemane, Peter's motives were tempered with the desire to protect his master and judge his enemies as they came to arrest him. On the surface it was a justifiable response, but Jesus, with his words and actions, shows us he desires to take us to another level. While the church runs around wielding the sword of judgement, maiming those believed to be Jesus' enemies, our Saviour commands us to put away our judgemental cutlasses and then visually demonstrates the way it should be done by reaching out and restoring his enemy's ear (see Jn. 18:10; Lk. 22:51).

Isn't it interesting that the analogy Jesus uses as we are sent with his life-giving message to the world is that of sheep amongst wolves and not the other way around? Do our unbelieving friends run when they see us coming? Perhaps it is because we mistakenly believe Jesus commissioned us as guard dogs, and we have religious foam dripping from our mouths, growling, snarling and snapping, defending instead of disarming! Philip Yancey in *What's so Amazing about Grace?* encapsulates the essence of what I'm trying to say in this chapter by telling a story of a prostitute who came to see a friend of Yancey's.

> A prostitute came to me in wretched straits, homeless, sick, unable to buy food for her two-year-old daughter. Through sobs and tears she told me she had been renting out her daughter, two years old, to men interested in kinky sex. She made more renting out her daughter for an hour than she could earn on her own in a night. She had to do it she said to support her own drug habit. I could hardly bear hearing her sordid story. For one thing, it made me legally liable. I'm required to report cases of child abuse. I had no idea what to say to this woman. At last I asked if she had ever thought of going to a Church for help. I will never forget the look of pure naive shock that crossed her face. 'Church!' she cried. 'Why would I ever go there? I was already feeling terrible about myself. They'd just make me feel worse.'

Yancey continues:

> What struck me about my friend's story is that women much like this prostitute fled towards Jesus not away from Him. The worse a person felt about herself, the more likely she saw Jesus as a refuge.

Yancey then poses the challenging question: 'Has the church lost that gift?'

If we want to be an edible church, tasty to the world and reflecting the goodness of God, there needs to be a marination in sacrifice. God exhorts us in Romans 12:1 to present ourselves to him as a living sacrifice. God is not asking us to present ourselves to him because he wants us to do sacrificial things. He's asking that we be the sacrifice. He wants us to die when no one else is prepared to in order for us to be the redeemer of situations. Francis Frangipane stated when we think of salvation 'we often see it through selfish eyes. When we accept Christ into our lives, it means not only that through our death we gain passage to Heaven, but also that in life Jesus gains passage to earth'.

Our salvation is not just about us. Our salvation gives Jesus flesh and blood all over again to bring mercy to our needy world.

Brian McLaren in his excellent book *A New Kind of Christian*[14] says:

> Church does not exist for the benefit of its members, it exists to equip its members for the benefit of the world. Church is not a place where we recruit people to be customers of our products or consumers of our religious programmes. We recruit them to be colleagues in our mission. The Church does not exist to satisfy the consumer demands of believers. The Church exists to equip and mobilise men and women for God's mission to the world. His mission is not to make more people more religious, but to make them more and more authentic.

We have to be careful the church does not become a recycling of Babel, where all the building and desire to touch heaven was not about God but all about them (see Gen. 11:4). Church is not about making a name for ourselves in order to play the 'Our church is bigger than your church' game. Has the spirit of 'keeping up with the Joneses' crept into the church? Are ministries motivated by jealousy or a desire for reputation? Church growth is not about comparison or competition, it's about sacrifice and compassion.

This is a day where not only the secular worships success, but when many of those of us in church leadership are guilty of the same offence. I know I certainly was, and still have the potential of falling into the trap. The test comes when God asks you for the success he has given you or removes it from you. He asked Abraham for the very vehicle through which he had promised prosperity – his son, Isaac. Abraham passed the test. God asked Philip to leave the furtherance of a revival, in which he was used as the catalyst, to other ministers. He passed the test, too. Very often it is failure, not success, that prepares a person's heart for usability.

The parable of the sower illustrates two kinds of test. Apart from the hard soil and the productive soil, there were two others – rocky soil and thorny soil. The rocky soil represents the enemies of affliction and persecution. The thorny soil represents the lure of materialism and money. The first test comes when things are too hard; the second test comes when things are too easy. Some people fail because of the pressure; some people give way under the prosperity.

McLaren again writes:

> The Church is not a human vacuum cleaner sucking up people from neighbourhoods so that they can be added to the membership role further enhancing the Church's image as being the biggest in the town. The Church is not about sucking people out of society to perpetuate itself. It's about blowing people back into society to be a blessing.

Our Church Mission Statement is three-fold.

1. To be church in our community
2. To build community in our church
3. To reach the world community through our church

Building community in the church is essential if we are to be church in our community. But this is not some introvert selfish enterprise. Community has three essential ingredients that will equip us to *be* church in the community. Again McLaren has helped me understand these three essential ingredients. The first one is 'Believing'. We all believe the same thing: the gospel of Jesus Christ. Believing it has transformed our lives. It's our common food, our yardstick, the spiritual oxygen we breathe and the foundation on which we build our lives. The second one is 'Belonging'. We create a place of belonging where people can learn more about the good news they have already believed. Thirdly, 'Behaviour'. This community desires to believe and live by what they are learning. The difference between Jesus and the religious system he continually exposed as being shallow and hypocritical is shoes and skin. Jesus was the Word incarnate, the truth in shoes, love in skin, whereas the Pharisees and religious leaders presented a spirituality that centred on temples, synagogues, rules and detachment. Maybe, much like the church you have known. McLaren writes:

> There is a new type of Church emerging with community controlling the life-flow. We meet together to believe and behave in order to become bread for a hungry world. We are to pray for and visually demonstrate the kingdom of God on earth lived out and demonstrated by those whose lives have been changed by it.

The church is a catalyst, not a goal; a barracks, not a five-star hotel; a battleship, not a cruise liner. God is sending us to classrooms, factories, offices, sports fields, theatres and next door neighbours to *be* church, to *be* bread for the hungry, to *be* edible so that they can taste and see that he is good.

When Oliver Cromwell needed extra gold and silver to mint more coins, he told his workers to go into the cathedrals and gather all the gold and silver statues of the saints, melt them down, and use the metal. His actual instructions were to melt down the saints and put them into circulation. The Holy Spirit is at work through his gifts, marinating his church with spices from heaven. Along with the spice of mercy and sacrifice come passion for his presence, obedience rather than preference, repentance not penance, grace and truth not religion and image, unity and community as opposed to division and competition, generosity, love and a host of others. The discovery of our tastelessness may come as a shock and not without some pain or disagreement but God loves the world too much to let people starve through lack of spiritual nourishment. For those with ears to hear let me challenge you to co-operate with the Holy Spirit to make you what he desires you to be.

An awakened conscience

If we are going to talk about judgement we must understand where it begins. Judgement begins in God's house – have a guess where he lives! (See 1 Pet. 4:17.) I was introduced to the writings of Dr Paul Brand through reading Philip Yancey. Dr Brand was a world-renowned hand surgeon and leprosy specialist until his death in 2003. His research on pain has helped prevent tens of thousands of amputations. When asked what his greatest contribution to sufferers of leprosy was, he said that his greatest gift to any leper was the gift of pain. What I didn't know was that leprosy is a disease which attacks the nerve endings in the body robbing it of the sensation of pain. Robbing the body of pain – surely that would be a blessing? Not to a leper. One of the reasons lepers lose limbs is because they can severely damage an arm or leg without even feeling the pain. They could hold red hot items and watch their flesh burn without a tinge of discomfort. Hence, Dr Brand's contribution to reduce amputations; the reintroduction of pain through stimulated nerve endings has brought joy to many a leper.

Leprosy in Scripture is likened to sin. What leprosy does in the natural, sin does in the spiritual. It attacks our spiritual nerve endings. It dulls the conscience so that you don't feel the pain. In other words, it dulls the conscience so you are open to harm without even knowing it. God's greatest gift to a Christian is the same as Dr Brand gave to his patients – the gift of pain, the gift of an awakened conscience; the gift of awakened spiritual nerve endings so we are able again to feel the pain of sin's effect upon God, others and ourselves. In order for us to be brought to a realisation of just how inedible we have become as a church to a hungry world, our conscience has to be reawakened and sensitised, and that can be painful. Imagine if the World Cup Final was played without a referee; imagine if our country was void of a police force … and imagine if our destiny was worked out without a conscience. That's why the habitual reading, meditating and application of God's Word is essential. He uses it to keep our conscience sensitive. The purpose of God's Word attacking the effects of leprosy in our life is to restore sensitivity to areas that need it. Paul explains the idea perfectly in Romans 7:7–9. (I particularly like these verses as they appear in the Living Bible.) So, God's gift to us to ensure a successful journey and to keep us edible and tasty is an awakened conscience, the gift of pain.

For David it came through a person. His conscience was awakened through the loving yet fearless confrontation of Nathan: 'You are the man!' (see 2 Sam. 12:7). For Peter it was a look (see Lk. 22:61). For Saul it was a word (see Acts 9:4).

For the prodigal it was a pig pen (Lk. 15:14–19). What is it for you? How is God trying to awaken your conscience?

In all four examples, it was painful to accept the truth but their pain was the proof that their conscience was awake and it became the means to prevent spiritual amputations.

Finally …

In his book *The Mantle of the Harlot*,[15] Ray Comfort beautifully describes how God uses his Word to awaken our conscience, through the analogy of the ten plagues of Egypt. Using the same thought with a little of my own literary embellishment, I pray these final words which close this chapter will help you understand that the pain which comes from a re-sensitised conscience is in no way meant to condemn you but to save you.

His Word will sometimes come to turn what was once pleasurable into a river of undrinkable blood. Once your conscience is awakened you no longer enjoy drinking of its pleasures. Through his Word he shows you what you worshipped with your time, money and affection was only filthy flies, devouring locusts and loathsome cold-blooded frogs. The bed of unbiblical sex becomes infected with lice and is no longer a desirable place to sleep. The Word hails its stones down and beats us with a tormented conscience so that we can't sleep at night or look people in the eye. The plague of boils so sensitises us to the touch we can no longer fellowship with the unfruitful works of darkness or sit in the seat of the scornful. Then comes the thick darkness, darkness that can be felt. The darkness of our world lived in compromise closes in around us until we cry out for the light of the glorious gospel and the Word that comes to kill that which we idolise, God's replacement in our lives, the firstborn of our affections, to bring us to the end of ourselves so we may start to live for him. The plagues are not pleasant but necessary. They are God's gift of pain to save us from destroying ourselves and marinate us to feed a hungry world.

9

A Grateful Heart

Someone once said, 'Authority is not what you know but what you've survived'.[16] If that is the case, then my wife should be a Five Star General. How she ever survived her childhood was a miracle. I have sat for hours listening to the traumatic experiences she suffered. I am amazed, not only at how she survived at all, but how she has turned out to be the happy contented grateful lover of God that she is today.

One particular experience she shared with me touched me so deeply it became the reason I felt I had to write this chapter. Sitting cross-legged one night in her Oslo home, having just experienced the joy of her new-found relationship with Jesus, she picked up her guitar and, using the few chords she knew, began to strum melodies of praise to God. Then in the midst of her adoration party, the door of her heart was kicked open, and a group of unwanted, uninvited gatecrashers forced their way into her mind, screaming: 'How can you worship a God who allowed your childhood to be stolen from you?' One by one in the living room of her thoughts, they recounted their sad stories of rejection, abuse and neglect. Their persistent continuing voices finally won Laila over, and her melody of praise began to turn into a funeral dirge of complaint and grief. Her open raised hands of adoration were now clenched in frustration and anger as the gatecrashers continued to fuel the false truth that God was to blame.

Suddenly into that room of mental torture walked the Giver of Peace with the real story. One by one, he silenced the voices of memories past and took Laila on a journey through the times in her childhood where death should have taken her but was not allowed to. Death through drowning, death through suffocation, death through freezing and one particular incident – when she was just eight years old – death through suicide.

Following a particularly nasty domestic incident, Laila ran to her room, knelt by her bed and cried out to Jesus to help her. In her child's mind, she fully expected Jesus to walk through the wall, take her in his arms and wipe away the tears. She waited for some indication that at least he would let her know he cared. She waited and waited, but heaven was silent and, from her child's perspective, uninterested in the private hell of a little eight-year-old. She got up from her bedside, walked outside her house into the busy truck route – a road that conveyed heavy thundering trucks, day and night. That in itself would have been scary but on this particular day a howling blizzard brought visibility down to a minimum. She knelt in the middle of the road, a little bundle of sadness, no taller than a table, just wanting the pain to go away. This, she thought, was the best way to do it.

After kneeling in the biting cold wind for a while, she heard a gentle voice behind her: 'Little girl, what are you doing here?' She turned around, looked up, and gazed into the tearful face of a bus driver, his bus just a few feet behind him, engine still running. To be able to see a small child in the middle of a blinding snowstorm, and then stop on those icy roads in time was a miracle. Jesus, in the presence of those gatecrashers still trying to justify their presence on that traumatic day, whispered: 'Laila, who do you think stopped the bus? Yes, your life was tough as a child; yes, you nearly died many times. But I was with you always. I was the best babysitter you ever had.' At that moment, the room of her mind was emptied of her negative, intrusive grace-robbers. The realisation of God's protective care through those awful years caused her to unclench her fists, and throw her arms in gratitude around the neck of the best babysitter in the world. The result of that encounter and revelation is an incredible heart of gratitude that has become the greatest motivational factor in her passion to reach the lost. I believe that living with the spirit of thankfulness is the master key to contentment and consistency in our Christian life.

Thankfulness

Thankfulness is a quality that saturated the life of Jesus. Even when he was about to face the most horrific experience of his life, he embraced it, armed with a Spirit of thankfulness. Luke 22:17 tells us, 'Then He took the cup, and gave thanks ...' The account also says, '... He took bread, [and] gave thanks ...' (v. 19). The secret to living a contented life is cultivating and practising the habit of thankfulness. Thankfulness keeps the goodness of God before our eyes when things seem bad. It is Satan's business to parade circumstantial and relational pictures before our minds, to convince us God is not good during tough times.

Directed by God, David was instructed to appoint a certain group of priests whose constant specific ministry was to give thanks to God (1 Chr. 16:4). Whether Israel was at war or at peace, whenever it was in prosperity or lack, the ministry of thanksgiving was to be carried out regardless, 24–7. In so doing, it kept the goodness of God before their eyes whatever the circumstantial climate.

The New Testament expects the priests of the church, which includes all of us, to do the same. Paul writes in 1 Thessalonians 5:18, 'In everything give thanks; for this is the will of God in Christ Jesus for you.' Want to know how to stay in the will of God when the sea of life gets rough? Live with a grateful heart. The Bible doesn't say give thanks *for* everything but *in* everything.

Thankfulness is also the key to the presence and the glory of God. Take time to read and meditate on Psalm 95:2, Psalm 100:4 and 2 Chronicles 5:13,14 to get these truths firmly established in your heart. Thankfulness is the key to the power of God. Two incredible miracles of Jesus were preceded by a simple declaration of thanks; these are the raising of Lazarus from the dead and the feeding of 5,000 people with five loaves of bread and two small fish.

In the case of Lazarus, it was 'Father, I thank You that You have heard Me' (Jn. 11:41b). Before the miracle of provision, Jesus simply gave thanks and then proceeded to distribute the broken bread and fish amongst the disciples to give to the hungry crowd – '... looking up to heaven, he gave thanks...' (Lk. 9:16, NIV). It's time to stop complaining about what you don't have to meet your needs and the needs of others, and start giving thanks for what you do have. You will be surprised at what will happen if you do. Increase is closely connected to a grateful heart. Consider these scriptures.

> Then out of them should proceed thanksgiving And the voice of those who make merry; I will multiply them, and they shall not diminish (Jer. 30:19).

*So continuing daily with one accord in the temple, and
breaking bread from house to house, they ate their food
with gladness and simplicity of heart, praising God and having
favour with all the people. And the Lord added to the church
daily those who were being saved* (Acts 2:46,47, my italics).

A grateful heart in the life of a pastor will save him time
and money spent attending church growth seminars or
trying to implement the latest church growth technique.
Likewise, thankfulness developed and practised in the
life of the believer is one of the most powerful tools we
possess. When used daily and deliberately it can transform
our lives dramatically.

Where are the nine?

During one of our summer holidays at our home in
Norway, I was invited to speak to a small group of
Lutheran Christians; the majority of them were farmers
or were connected to a farming family. They are a loving,
helpful, private people who live with a strong sense of
community, and great respect and commitment to the
family, both 'nuclear' and extended. While these qualities
are to be admired, the privacy concerning their faith had
to be addressed. I asked the Holy Spirit what he wanted
me to teach, and immediately I heard the words, 'The
power of a grateful heart.' While meditating for a few
moments on this theme, another phrase began to dance
around in my thoughts; a phrase that demanded my
attention. It was this: 'Where are the nine?' Knowing
this was a statement made by Jesus after the healing of
the ten lepers, I turned to Luke 17 and read the story.
Sensitive as to how the Holy Spirit wanted to apply the
story to these private Christians, I slowly took in the
details of this amazing miracle. What I discovered were

three powerful ingredients of thankfulness I had never seen before.

Thankfulness – keeping connected

Firstly, I noticed that of the ten lepers only one came back to say thank you. Nine lepers appreciated what Jesus did for them I'm sure, but never came back to thank him. The thought hit me: you can appreciate Jesus from a distance but thankfulness keeps you coming back, staying close. Thankfulness is one of the main ingredients that will keep you connected to the Source of your salvation.

Thankfulness – making you whole

The second thing I noticed is that thankfulness makes you whole. We see in verse 19 of the account that Jesus said to the man, 'Arise, go your way. Your faith has made you well.'

Nine were cleansed but only one was pronounced well – or *whole*. In my ministry as a pastor, I see many who receive a healing or a deliverance from Jesus, but remain lukewarm, backslidden, or even return completely to their lifestyle prior to conversion. Spiritual erosion begins when there is an absence of gratitude. Thankfulness is the key to wholeness. It not only keeps you connected but consistent.

Thankfulness – making the private public

Yet for me it was the third principle I shared with these wonderful Norwegian farmers that struck a chord within regarding the power of a grateful heart. It was simply this: thankfulness has to make public that which was private. The story about my wife, with which I opened this chapter, highlights this aspect of thanksgiving – one that is sometimes overlooked. My wife is the most enthusiastic, passionate, personal communicator of her faith of anyone I know. Her thankfulness to God for the gift of salvation compels her to make public that which is private.

The one leper went beyond private appreciation to a public declaration of praise. He was grateful and he wanted everyone to know it. We are told that '... with a *loud voice* ... [he] fell ... at His feet, giving Him thanks ...' (Lk. 17:15,16). You can't get more public than that. What was said to those Norwegian Christians, who wanted to live their Christian lives privately, Jesus says to Christians worldwide. It's time to go public. This world will never be reached with the gospel because of our praying and believing, but by going public about what we pray and believe in private. Have we forgotten that we are containers of the Holy Spirit, not designed for storage but usage? When we think of our salvation we often see it through selfish eyes. Paul said '... it is no longer I who live, but Christ lives in me ...' (Gal. 2:20). As Frances Frangipane stated in *The Power of One Christ-like Life*:

> When we accept Christ into our lives, it means not only at death we gain passage to Heaven, but also that in life Jesus gains passage to earth. Our salvation is not just about us; our salvation gives Jesus flesh and blood all over again to bring mercy to our needy world.

Awesome!

I believe Charles Spurgeon once said that a little faith would take you to heaven, but that he prayed for the sort of faith that would bring heaven to earth. We have received Christ. We have received the power and presence of God, and it's not for private use. When we become grateful for what we have received, it is the match that lights the fuse that ignites the explosive that blows the gates marked 'Private! Keep out!' off its hinges and allows Christ's life to flow out to a desperate world. The words of Jesus to his disciples, as they were poised in the starting blocks of their mission to the world, were '... you shall *receive* power ...' (see Acts 1:8, my italics). He didn't say, 'you shall *release* power'. For that to happen there has to be a willing co-operation on our part. God has done his part; it is now our responsibility to activate that divine life deposited within us and disperse it to a hungry world. The power that resides within us, through the indwelling Christ, is latent power. It is potential power; power that needs to be activated. The power of a battery has to be activated; to watch your favourite TV programme you have to tune in; to release the power of dynamite you have to light the fuse. The question is 'How do we activate the life of Christ and release his potential power within us to change our world?' These are five simple steps. Use them and watch your life turn from a dialling tone to a full-scale concert.

Doing

The first step is 'Doing'. We read in Acts 10:38 that '... God anointed Jesus of Nazareth with the Holy Spirit and with power, who went about *doing* good ...' (my italics). Jesus never said, 'I love you' to anyone. He didn't need to. He went around *doing* love. While we clamour for some new charismatic experience, selfishly desiring what we believe is some spiritual ladder giving us brownie points in heaven and making us feel good, many in our circle of influence are crying out for simple acts of kindness. Jesus didn't go around *feeling* good, but *doing* good. There are many who will sacrifice life and limb to get to some meeting where they believe heavenly experiences are being poured out, but cannot walk across the street to help their neighbour in times of crisis. The power and anointing of God belongs to the obedient, not simply the informed or spiritually experienced. The life of Christ within us is released when we do the Word, not simply hear it or feel it; read James 1:22!

Being

The second step is that of 'Being'. Isn't it interesting that the principles laid out by Jesus in his classic 'Sermon on the Mount' are called *Be*atitudes? Be humble. Be teachable. Be passionate. Be merciful. Be pure. Be a peacemaker. Be consistent under pressure. The hardened Roman centurion, who participated in the gruesome death of Jesus, was convinced of Jesus' divinity simply because of Jesus' authenticity. He had probably heard him speak, and maybe seen him perform a miracle or two. But it was his observation of how Jesus reacted with forgiveness towards his persecutors that won his heart. 'Truly this Man was the Son of God!' (Mk. 15:39b) was not a revelation based on the spectacular but the authentic. God is love, and his Son willingly and visually became it.

Let me tell you a story that encapsulates the essence of 'Being' a follower of Christ. The scene is a courtroom trial in South Africa. An elderly black lady rises to her feet. Facing her are a number of white police officers – one of them Mr Van der Broek. He has just been tried and found to be implicated in the murders of the lady's son and husband. This man had come to the lady's home, taken her son and shot him, then set the body on fire. Some time later, Van der Broek and his men came back for the lady's husband and for months she didn't know anything of his whereabouts. Almost two years after his disappearance, Van der Broek came to fetch the lady herself. She was taken to a place beside a river and shown her husband, bound and beaten, lying on a pile of wood. His last words, as the police officer poured gasoline over his body and set him alight, were 'Father, forgive them.'

Now that lady stands in the courtroom listening to the confessions of Mr Van der Broek. A member of South Africa's Truth and Reconciliation Commission turns to her. He asks her what she wants, and how justice should be done to the man who so brutally destroyed her family.

The lady replies that she wants three things. She wants to be taken to the place where her husband's body had been burned so she can gather the dust and give his remains a decent burial. Then she stopped before she continued. She said that her husband and son were her only family. So her second request was that Mr Van der Broek would become her son. She asked that he would come twice a month to spend a day with her so she could lavish her love on him. She also wanted a third thing. She said it was also the wish of her husband. What was that third thing? That someone would lead her across the courtroom so she could embrace Mr Van der Broek and let him know he was truly forgiven.

As the court assistants came to help the elderly lady across the room, Van der Broek fainted, completely overwhelmed. As he did so, people in the courtroom – family, neighbours and friends, all victims of years of injustice and oppression – began to sing *Amazing Grace*.[17]

Speaking

The third step to release the life of Christ, latent but powerful within us, is 'Speaking' – 'But sanctify the Lord God in your hearts, and always be ready to give a defence to everyone who asks you a reason for the hope that is in you, with meekness and fear' (1 Pet. 3:15). When the world we live in is so vocal about what it believes, the people sometimes unashamedly vocal about the way they live, brazenly revealing with pride their shameful private lives, why should it be that so often Christians are too embarrassed even to mention the name of Jesus in public? The foolishness of preaching is still God's method to make available his life-changing power to anyone who will believe it.

Touching

The fourth principle that activates God's power within is 'Touching'. Jesus astonished the religious leaders of his day by touching the untouchable. Steve Chalke in his book *The Lost Message of Jesus*[18] tells of this incident in the life of the late Princess Diana, when she visited an AIDS hospital in central London back in 1985.

> Back then little was known about HIV and AIDS, and as a result a huge amount of suspicion and fear surrounded those who were infected. Despite reassurances from the medical profession that it was virtually impossible to catch this terrible and incurable disease from minor contact with a patient, the majority of the population still worried that they were in danger of catching the deadly virus if they so much as touched someone who was HIV positive, drank from the same cup or even breathed the same air. According to the popularly held view, Diana was running a high risk of becoming HIV positive herself.
>
> Ignorance led to intolerance and intolerance led to prejudice. Waitresses lost their jobs when customers discovered they were HIV positive. Children with infected parents were taken out of schools, and local leaders had to hide the fact that people with AIDS were living in their towns. AIDS became the leprosy of the late twentieth century as its victims encountered rejection, discrimination,

intolerance and social isolation. Some were even denied basic human rights, such as liberty, autonomy, security and freedom of movement.

Deliberately and in front of the invited TV cameras, Diana sat down on a bed next to a young homosexual dying of AIDS. She took hold of his hand and talked to him. This calculated and brave action and the worldwide media attention it attracted became a prophetic act that was to challenge popular perception. Diana's simple example of acceptance caused people around the world to rethink their attitudes. It undermined a common worldview about AIDS and as a result changed the lives of millions of people who had previously been shunned by the communities in which they lived.

The Bible encourages us to touch people. It seems it is another way in which God disperses his life through us into others (read Mk. 8:22; 10:13; 16:18). In the process of ministering to those Norwegian farmers, a man came to be healed of a tumour on his brain. My wife and I simply obeyed the command to lay hands on the sick and left the outcome with God. As a result the man is back in work, his sisters have become believers and the word spread around the community there were 'healers' in their midst. People started coming to our house or requesting we visit them, and we have seen Jesus do wonderful miracles of healing and salvation simply because we obeyed his command to 'touch' people in his name.

Going

The fifth key to release this latent indwelling power of Christ is 'Going'. Nothing happens unless someone goes. Therefore it must be time to take his life into dead situations, his love into sadness, his light into darkness, and disperse his power into the impossible. Before we experience the miraculous promised in Mark 16:17,18 ('And these signs will follow those who believe: In My name they will cast out demons; they will speak with new tongues; they will take up serpents; and if they drink anything deadly, it will by no means hurt them; they will lay hands on the sick, and they will recover.'), we have to obey the command of verse 15. We must '... *Go* into all the world and preach the gospel to every creature' (my italics).

Finally ...

As wonderful and practical as all these principles are, the key to it all becoming a reality is a grateful heart.

My childhood, in contrast to Laila's, was a very happy one. We were three brothers, a sister, a dog, and a cat with no teeth. My father was a hardworking man and, even though he had no Christian faith, he did have good family values, and loved us all in his own way. My mother was amazing. On top of taking care of a family of four, and being a great wife to my father, she also brought in extra money through the three jobs she held. Two were cleaning jobs, and the third consisted of peeling potatoes in the local fish and chip shop. Day after day cleaning and scouring floors and peeling potatoes can really take its toll on your hands and, of all the things I remember about my mother, her hands were the most memorable. They weren't pretty to look at or nice to hold. They were tough, like sandpaper. Sometimes they were so cracked and hard they would split open and start to bleed. They often became so sensitive she couldn't hold a spoon to stir her tea.

Every Saturday night we would be permitted to stay up late to watch TV, because my mother would be allowed to bring home what the fish shop didn't sell. Saturday night for us was feast night. Sausage rolls, fish, pies and my favourite – chicken. On one particular Saturday night we were all waiting with hungry bellies. 'Mam' came through the door with her usual bulging newspaper parcel holding the greasy, tasty supper. She opened the paper and to my horror, no chicken! How could she? My mother knew I loved chicken. I was so disappointed, and I let everyone know just how much. But while I was ungratefully looking at the newspaper, containing everything but the chicken I wanted, I forgot to look at and appreciate the blistered, cracked hands that held the paper. With those tired, cracked hands, she cared for us, provided for us and protected us, but because of ungratefulness, I failed to appreciate their worth.

The next time Jesus blesses you with a gift – relational, spiritual or financial – take the time to look at his hands. They speak volumes of how much he sacrificed so you and I could be blessed. I can't say thank you to my mother any more as she is no longer with us, but I'm not going to make the same mistake with Jesus. The look of disappointment on my mother's face because of my ungratefulness stings my heart much more than the sting of the toasting fork against my rump when I misbehaved.

I believe the biggest disappointment in Jesus' heart today as he looks at his church, is not our lack of power, gifting or influence, but a lack of gratitude. He still says those four words, after lifting us when we're down, directing us when we're confused, providing for us when we're in need, healing us when we are sick: 'Where are the nine?'

10

The Confident Heart

There is a story told concerning an incident in the life of Charles Spurgeon.[19] Called to visit one of his parishioners who was dying he arrived at her home, and was shocked at her living conditions. It was a one-room accommodation and the epitome of poverty; no furnishings, no carpets – just a bed, a table and pieces of old cloth hanging over the windows giving her some privacy. The walls were bare except for one picture frame. Spurgeon walked over to this lone piece of decoration and studied the slip of paper within the frame. He asked the lady how she came by this particular possession.

'Mr Spurgeon,' she replied, 'many years ago I worked for a very wealthy woman, and I was her maid. I did everything for her, not merely out of duty, I really loved her. We had a great relationship. Sometimes, I forgot I was the maid and that she was the employer; she also suffered from the same lapse of memory. We were almost like sisters. Sadly, she died, but while on her deathbed, as I am now, she handed me the piece of paper you see framed on the wall. I've treasured it ever since. I have never been able to read, and I was too embarrassed to ask anyone to read it for me. So, I framed it and placed it on the wall. Every time I look at it, I am reminded of the great times we had together.'

Spurgeon paused, still stunned by what he had discovered by reading the piece of paper, and now the story behind it.

'Lady, that piece of paper which you couldn't read, is a cheque for a considerable amount of money, which makes you one of the richest women in the neighbourhood. All these years you have been living in abject poverty when you could have been living in comfort, and also have plenty left over to help many others. All because you could not read and understand what was written on that piece of paper.'

How many Christians are living way below standard, emotionally, spiritually, relationally and even financially, all because they don't understand what's rightfully theirs in Christ? Hosea 4:6 informs us that God's own people are perishing because of a lack of understanding of what they're entitled to – 'My people are destroyed for lack of knowledge' (v. 6a). There are so many Christians missing out because they really don't understand, apply and receive the blessing God wants them to have. For too long many have been standing back when it comes to receiving from God. The reason, simply put – they don't know *how* to receive. For example, we pray as instructed by Jesus: 'your kingdom come, your will be done on earth as it is in heaven' (Mt. 6:10, NIV). We get disappointed when in reality we don't see that happen; we blame everyone and everything, including God, instead of reading and applying the instructions that precede the statement. His kingdom is within us and available to us, but it is not experienced automatically.

There are, as far as I can determine, four elements that have to be in place before the dynamics of the kingdom of heaven can operate.

Unity

Firstly the principle of unity has to be found and applied. Jesus said, 'In this manner, therefore, pray ...' (Mt. 6:9a). In other words, 'I am giving you specific instruction on how to pray in order to receive maximum results. Start by saying "Our Father", not "*Your* Father" or "*My* Father", but "*Our* Father".' You cannot pray like that while at the same time harbouring a spirit of independence. To pray 'Our' means you understand it's not just about you. There is no such thing as lone Christianity. When it comes to the kingdom of God we don't pray 'My Father', we pray 'Our Father'. I believe this type of prayer is different to the type of prayer Jesus spoke of in Matthew 6:5–8, where he encourages us to go into our private place and seek God out of the gaze of a watching world. Here he is emphasising the shallowness of the pharisaic prayer; the one that likes to be seen and heard, the one that feeds off the praise of others. But in what we refer to as 'The Lord's Prayer', I believe the emphasis is not on privacy but on unity. We have to come together to pray a prayer like that, or pray with a spirit of unity in our hearts.

I have heard that Joyce Meyer said, humorously, that she prayed in perfect unity when she was at home, as long as she was on her own. As soon as other people came on the scene, that was the end of her unity! Living with a spirit of unforgiveness, spite or revenge prevents the kingdom of God being a reality in our lives. So, in effect, we're stumped at first base. If you can't get beyond 'Our' you have a problem, and need to get it sorted if you want to experience 'your kingdom come'.

Relationship

The second element is Relationship – 'Our Father', not our set of rules, not our religion, not our liturgy, but our Father. I know it seems ridiculous, but there are many who relate to God as anything but Father. Some know him as Master, some as Lord, some possibly as employer, but his passion for us is that we know him as Father. It's imperative, if we want to experience God's 'kingdom come' in our lives.

At the beginning of the parable of the talents, Jesus informs his listeners, who want to know how the kingdom of God operates, 'For the kingdom of heaven is like …' (Mt. 25:14). He proceeds to tell the parable which includes the servant who buried his talent: 'Then he who had received the one talent came and said, "Lord, I knew you to be a hard man, reaping where you have not sown, and gathering where you have not scattered seed. And I was afraid, and went and hid your talent in the ground"' (Mt. 25:24,25a). Why did the servant in the parable of the talents bury the only one he was given? The parable reveals the answer. He had a warped perception of the one who entrusted it to him. The reason for this man's unproductiveness boiled down to a bad relationship. He saw his master as a 'hard man'; so deep was this perception ingrained into him, he was also very much 'afraid' of him.

We are never going to receive anything from someone we perceive as being hard or someone we run away from or hide things from because we are afraid of their reaction. The 'relationship' thing has to be sorted before we can experience the power of God's kingdom in our lives. When the prodigal returned from the pig sty, he was happy just to be a servant. His mentality centred on the fact that he could not be treated as a son after what he had done and where he had been. However, on his return, the father immediately re-established the relational foundation between himself and the returning prodigal. The father could have remarked, 'You may not look like my son, but the fact remains I have never stopped being your father. I was your father when you lived here. I was your father when you decided to leave. I was your father when you were in the pig sty, and I am your father now.'

How many times, because of some bad decision that took us away from the purposes of God, and our Father's house, have we messed up and returned with the mentality of a prodigal – 'I am no longer worthy to be called your son'? When are we going to get it? He has never stopped being a Father! '... Bring out the best robe and put it on him, and put a ring on his hand and sandals on his feet. And bring the fatted calf here and kill it, and let us eat and be merry; for this my *son* was dead and is alive again ...' (see Lk. 15:22–24, my italics).

That's why Satan continually tries to sow doubt in your heart concerning your sonship. There is a lot at stake. Servants are not entitled to the same privileges sons are. We all visit pig sties and come back stinking, feeling unworthy to enjoy the privileges of a son and Satan knows this and capitalises on our sense of uncleanness. He even challenged Jesus in the wilderness over this important issue, as we have already seen. His attack opened with '*If* You are the Son of God' (Lk. 4:3, my italics). Satan immediately went for one of the central issues that govern the release of kingdom blessings – the relationship. 'Are you sure God is your Father? Are you sure you are his Son? Was that voice you heard at the River Jordan a figment of your imagination? No one has ever called God Father – what makes you so different?' Sound familiar? If he tried it with Jesus, he will try it with you.

I have no doubt in my mind I belong to the Bevan family. Never once have I doubted the fact I am a Bevan. On good days or bad days my conviction remains consistent. In fact, I never give it a thought because if challenged legally, all I have to do is produce my birth certificate. It proves beyond doubt that I am a Bevan. Why don't you do that with your relationship with your heavenly Father when Satan accuses you concerning your relationship? When Satan tries to convince you God is a 'hard man' who blesses you based on your performance, and he tries to sow doubt in your mind, as he did with Jesus, that God may not be your Father, pull out your birth certificate and read it to him: 'But as many as received Him, to them [that means you if you have received Christ], He gave the right to become children of God, to those who believe in His name' (Jn. 1:12).

Look at these scriptures from 1 John 5:11–15: 'And this is the testimony: that God has given us eternal life, and this life is in His Son. He who has the Son has life; he who does not have the Son of God does not have life. These things I have written to you who believe in the name of the Son of God *that you may know* that you have eternal life ...' (my italics); 'Now this is the confidence' – what is? Being sure about who you're related to, 'that if we ask anything according to His will, He hears us. And if we know that He hears us, whatever we ask, we know that we have the petitions that we have asked of Him.' Fantastic! Before the blessings of the kingdom of heaven can be expected with confidence, the relationship issue has to be settled. You are his child, he is your Father. Believe it and act upon it, and by faith begin to live in it.

Sovereignty

The third essential element needed before we can command God's kingdom come, is sovereignty: 'Our Father *in heaven*' (Mt. 6:9, NIV, my italics). For God's kingdom to operate in our lives on a daily basis there must be an absolute conviction that God lives in a place of total authority and your life is hidden with him, in Christ in heaven. Satan will attack 'our' with disunity and strife. He will attack 'Father' with condemnation. And he will attack 'in heaven' with worry.

The secret for the Early Church having their prayers answered was their absolute belief that whatever happened *to* them, whatever was happening *around* them, their God, their Father, was in complete control. In the midst of intense persecution and threat to their lives, they knew exactly who he was and where he was: '... they raised their voice to God with one accord and said: "Lord, You are God, who made heaven and earth and the sea, and all that is in them"' (Acts 4:24). Their weapon against worry and fear was the revelation and conviction that God was Sovereign and ruling from heaven.

Jesus encourages us to live the same way – 'Our Father in heaven'. Circumstances don't rule your life, heaven does. The economy doesn't rule your life, heaven does. In Mel Gibson's *The Passion of the Christ*, depicting graphically the last 24 hours of Jesus' life on earth, it did not look as if heaven was in control at all. It appeared Jesus was a man who was manifestly not in control of his own destiny, the centrepiece of a satanically controlled event, all the morality of humankind gone wild. Yet in the middle of it all, his words to Pilate give us the reason for his endurance and confidence. 'Then Pilate said to Him, "Are You not speaking to me? Do You not know that I have power to crucify You, and power to release You?" Jesus answered, "You could have no power at all against Me unless it had been given you from above...."' (Jn. 19:10,11). In other words, 'My Father is in heaven. That means he pulls the strings.'

What or who is Pilate in your life, arrogantly asserting they are in control?

Hallowed be your name

Find someone to agree with you in prayer and pray 'our'. Settle the issue of sonship and continue to pray 'Father'. Establish firmly in your heart the conviction of Sovereignty, 'in heaven'. Then the fourth element will be released automatically – 'hallowed be your name'. Worship, thanksgiving and praise ... do it, now!

Finally ...

As you praise and worship, do so with boldness, based on your revelation of unity, sonship, trust and thanksgiving; command 'God's kingdom' to come into your situation. He wants it to happen more than you do, because kingdom is at the centre of his heart.

11

The Failed Heart

If ever you're planning to learn how to ski, I want to save you a lot of disappointment by telling you up front – in the process of learning, you are going to fall. I haven't heard of anyone who has taken up skiing that hasn't fallen. Not just on one occasion, but numerous times, before they felt confident enough to attempt a difficult slope – they fell. I even know of proficient skiers that, either through a lapse of concentration or the irresponsibility of others still suffered injury through a fall they didn't really expect.

When I started to learn to ski, not only did I fall many times in the process, but when I fell, I had to endure the ridicule of a group of three- to ten-year-olds. I had successfully negotiated the children's slope (after many attempts), only to face the added challenge of getting back up to the top again. The means was a technical contraption – the ski lift. This, I knew, had to be treated with wisdom and respect for it had the potential to damage me for life. There was a continuous moving wire loop, with occasional pieces of wood hanging from it, and fixed to the end of each one was what seemed to be a seating area no larger than a saucepan lid. The idea was that you grabbed this moving stick with perfect timing, placed the saucepan lid between your legs, and off you went.

I stood in line, towering above my little comrades – those miniature experts who were making the whole thing look easy. I observed how they skilfully negotiated the moving saucepan lids … whilst at the same time trying to concentrate on remaining in an upright position. I nearly fell a few times while shuffling my skis closer to the lift as the line in front of me got smaller. Finally, I was next. There was a line of about twenty to thirty children behind me. All eyes were fixed in anticipation of what might happen.

I didn't disappoint them. I grabbed hold of one of the poles and attempted to emulate my little mentors. I really don't know what happened next; everything became a blur. Suddenly I found myself hanging on for dear life as I was dragged up the hill, skis and sticks flying in all directions to the amusement and side-splitting laughter of my audience.

So let me warn you. Not only are you going to fall learning to ski, you're going to look stupid in the process. You're also going to feel helpless and there is a strong possibility you're going to get hurt.

I eventually managed to stand up and stay up for longer than ten minutes, and grappled with and mastered the technique of the ski lift. Then my friends encouraged me to try a real slope. After convincing me it was as easy as the children's slope, only longer, I agreed to try it. When I arrived at the start of the run and stood looking down at what seemed to be the side of Mount Everest, I knew immediately I'd been tricked. Before I knew it, I was careering down a red slope at what felt like hundreds of miles an hour, screaming the name of Jesus and confessing my sin. How I reached the halfway mark without falling I don't know, but amazingly I did.

'OK,' said my friend, appealing to my freshly swelled ego. 'For the last part of the hill don't slalom, tuck your ski sticks under your arms and go straight down.'

'Do you think I can?' I asked.

'Well, you made it this far without falling! Go for it.'

I did. For the first fifty yards or so I was fine, but as I gathered speed my skis began to shake violently and seemed to have a mind of their own. One wanted to go right, and the other wanted to go left. The rest of my body wanted to go straight on, but my skis had made their decision and I could do nothing to stop them. The next thing I knew I was looking at the sky and wondered why I was experiencing the sensation of flying. It was because I was now completely out of contact with the snow and was horizontal to the slope travelling at thirty or forty miles an hour. When I landed, I felt I had been dropped from a four-storey building onto concrete. I completed the run sliding down the slope looking like a dead starfish. My head hurt for days after, along with every other bone in my body.

Please take a lesson from my experience; if you're going to ski, you're going to fall. *When* you fall, not *if* you fall, you're going to look stupid, you're going to feel helpless and you're definitely going to get hurt. Do you know something else I've learned? Life is just the same!

Failure

As you work out your salvation, as you work out your destiny, there are times when you are going to fall, make mistakes, fail at something. When you do, you're going to look stupid, feel helpless and get hurt. But the great thing is – your failures, embarrassments, helplessness and hurts can end up being wonderful teachers. I didn't let the results of my falls stop me skiing. I learned from them. I have approached my life, mistakes, failures and disappointments in the same way. Failure is part of life. We are going to make mistakes, sometime, at something.

Everyone wants the reputation of having integrity, but often we confuse integrity with perfection. Many feel failure robs them of integrity, not realising it has nothing to do with performance, but everything to do with character. Learn to embrace failure as a teacher, not an undertaker. The important thing is not what happens to you or around you but *in* you. You can't control the length of your life, but you can control its width and its depth. No matter how experienced a skier you are, you still have the potential to fall. No matter how experienced you are as a Christian, you still have the potential to fail at something.

A lesson from the life of Moses

How would you feel if God personally carved two tablets of granite from the side of a mountain, wrote very important instructions on them with his own hand, then gave them to you for safe keeping? Along with this precious gift you were told the instructions written on them were to be given to help guide, govern and guard a whole nation. Pretty serious, don't you agree? Wouldn't you say these tablets of stone were so unique, so special and important that you would treat them with great respect and guard them with your life? But imagine if you broke them in pieces on purpose. How would you feel, and more importantly, how do you think God would feel?

Well, this is not just a scenario, it actually happened. God had spent 80 years preparing his servant Moses to lead his people out of the clutches of a tyrannical regime, preparing him for the moment when he would experience what no other person had experienced. He was entrusted with something no other person had ever held in their hands. But in one brief lapse of self-control, he blew it. We've all broken the Ten Commandments, but not one of us has done it literally. Moses did. However justified Moses' anger was, in response to the rebellion, idolatry and downright disrespect of God's people to their deliverer, what Moses did was unforgivable. Or was it?

Exodus 32:15–19 says: 'And Moses turned and went down from the mountain, and the two tablets of the Testimony were in his hand. The tablets were written on both sides; on the one side and on the other they were written. Now the tablets were the work of God, and the writing was the writing of God engraved on the tablets. And when Joshua heard the noise of the people as they shouted, he said to Moses, "There is a noise of war in the camp." But he said: "It is not the noise of the shout of victory, Nor the noise of the cry of defeat, But the sound of singing I hear." So it was, as soon as he came near the camp, that he saw the calf and the dancing. So Moses' anger became hot, and he cast the tablets out of his hands and broke them at the foot of the mountain.'

If Indiana Jones had been there, he would have been diving – even at the threat to his life – to save something so unique; imagine two tablets of stone, with God's handwriting, irreplaceable, priceless, one of a kind! But '... Moses' anger became hot, and he cast the tablets out of his hands ...' *And he broke them!* AAAAAAAARRRRR RGGGGGGHHH!

Moses, how could you? But he did. However spiritual you think you are, you still have the potential within you to break something God has entrusted to you. The presence of God or the most intense spiritual experience does not eliminate our potential to fail. Read Exodus 24:12–18. Here the account is given of Moses being supernaturally sustained for 40 days and 40 nights by simply being in the physical presence of God. But even after that he still couldn't control his temper. Wow!

One thing I've discovered as I have desired to fulfil my calling and destiny, and that is, my humanity will always be a limitation to my God-given assignment. Hudson Taylor said that all God's people were weak people. But it didn't prevent God using them in spite of the flaws in their humanity. Gideon's weakness was his self-esteem and deep insecurities, but God transformed him into a mighty man of valour. Abraham's weakness was his fear. Twice he claimed his wife was his sister to protect himself. But God transformed him into 'the father of all those who believe' (Rom. 4:11). Peter's weakness was his impulsiveness and unreliability, but he became known as the Rock. Moses' weakness was his temper and in one uncontrolled moment, he broke something precious given to him by God. But there is something about our failure and God's response to it that you must learn from this incident if you're going to finish your race. God did not write Moses off, he simply rewrote the plan on that which Moses brought to him after he paid the consequences for his failure. You see, God doesn't deny our failure took place. He doesn't wink at our sins. He demands we face up to them and take the consequences but at the same time, if a repentant honest heart is found, he can rewrite his destiny on such a one, so they can continue their journey.

'And the LORD said to Moses, "Cut two tablets of stone like the first ones, and I will write on these tablets the words that were on the first tablets *which you broke*"' (Ex. 34:1, my italics).

I almost want to laugh and cry at the same time when I read this verse. On the one hand, Moses had to take the consequences of his failure by using his energy to re-cut two stone tablets out of the hard rock on Mount

Sinai. Perhaps realising just how difficult that was, he would probably pay them more respect. He presented them to God, and God simply rewrote the original plan on those second pair of tablets. That makes me want to cry! How many times have I broken what God has given to me? I know I've broken his heart many times, but still he forgives as I learn my lesson through repentance and consequence. Then, because of his incredible mercy, he passionately rewrites his original plan for my life on the spiritual tissue of my heart, which is now softer and hopefully a lot wiser.

What is it that God has entrusted to you and, for whatever reason, you've treated with contempt or irresponsibility or ended up breaking? Is it a relationship he gave you? A marriage? A ministry? A dream? A family? A job? Whatever it is, failure is not the end if you look at the example of Moses. Stop blaming. Stop denying. Stop regretting. Accept the consequences and allow God to rewrite his predestined plan on your life again.

'So he cut two tablets of stone like the first ones. Then Moses rose early in the morning and went up Mount Sinai, as the LORD had commanded him; and he took in his hand the two tablets of stone. Now the LORD descended in the cloud and stood *with* him there [not against him] and proclaimed the name of the LORD. And the LORD passed before him and proclaimed, "The LORD, the LORD God, *merciful and gracious, longsuffering, and abounding in goodness and truth, keeping mercy for thousands, forgiving iniquity and transgression and sin"'* (Ex. 34:4–7a, my italics). Wow! Moses walked right into the presence of God with the evidence of his failure in his hand; the evidence of his repentant heart, the evidence of his acceptance of consequence represented by the re-cut tablets of stone. And God just started to shout love not judgement at him. Moses walked straight into a cloud of mercy and had his destiny rewritten.

While reeling from the effects of a personal failure, trying to deal with both pain and arrogance at the same time, someone gave me a framed poem by Rudyard Kipling, called *If*. It helped me to get myself correctly orientated. I do urge you to get a hold of a copy and read it through, and I pray it will help you as much as it helped me.

Finally ...

For some reading these words, the Father calls to you with the same passion and desire. Failure is part of life. Accept that or live with delusion. But failure is not the end of life. You must know how to walk into his cloud of mercy on a daily basis; otherwise you will never make it. There is a journey to the centre of his heart that he has clearly marked out.

In *The Wizard of Oz*, the only thing Dorothy had to do to get to her destination was to follow the yellow brick road. God has a Red Brick Road coloured by his blood that leads you to a place where destinies are rewritten. I've been there a number of times to have him rewrite mine. I know the embarrassing consequences of a fall. I know what it feels like to look stupid before a watching world, to feel helpless to defend or help myself. I know what it is to be hurting, wondering 'Will I ever attempt ministry again?' But I discovered the Red Brick Road. The same road Moses trod to have God rewrite his destiny.

Come on; let me take you on a journey to the centre of his heart. I know the way.

12

Journey to Centre of His Heart

I was sitting at my desk one afternoon when the door to my study flew open, followed by hysterical shouts from my then six-year-old son, Carl.

'Daddy, Daddy! Can I have money for an ice cream? The ice cream van is outside! He won't stay long. Quick, quick, I need money *now*!'

Although it could appear that my son's request was, on the surface, a very selfish one, I had to believe it was based more on urgency than selfishness. Here he was, a small boy in a crisis. The ice cream van was outside. The opportunity to buy an ice cream was passing by. The urgency of the situation demanded radical action. There was no fear in his heart about invading my privacy without knocking, because I was his dad; I would understand. He was a little boy with a need and I was his father with the means to meet that need. I promptly gave him the money, and he shot out of the room even faster than he'd entered.

As he was leaving the room, I heard these words deep inside me: 'Ray, why can't you be like that with me?

Imagine,' the voice continued, 'if your son, in his need, knocked the door to your study and heard a thundering, threatening voice from inside growling "Who is it? What do you want? Can't you hear I'm busy?"

'Your son begins to shake outside, picturing an angry, upset, unwilling person called "Father" letting him know even before he enters the room he's not welcome. The person from whom he is seeking help is not happy at all. His privacy has been disturbed and he has just started off completely on the wrong foot. The door creaks open, your six-year-old son falls prostrate on the floor and begins to crawl across the floor, all the while demeaning himself with self-depreciating comments like, "I'm just a worm, Oh Almighty, Omnipresent One, I am not worthy to be in the same room as you and based on my behaviour and performance as a son this week, I certainly don't feel I have the right to ask this request, but please can I have money for an ice cream?" As he grovels, shivering with fear in your presence, awaiting an answer, he covers his face with his arm to protect himself from the blow he's expecting for having the audacity to be so bold to ask his dad for ice-cream money.

'How would you feel, Ray?' the voice insisted. 'As one father to another, please tell me how you would feel.'

I answered from deep inside: 'I would feel terrible to think of my son having to approach me like that; for him to come into my presence expecting a fist not an embrace would make me very sad.'

My heavenly Father then whispered to me again (by now I knew who it was speaking to me). 'How do you think I feel when my kids approach me like that? The way your son approached you for an ice cream is the way I've been telling my kids to approach me. Go tell my kids they can "come boldly to the throne of grace, [to] obtain mercy and find grace to help [them] in time of need"' (Heb. 4:16).

The journey to the centre of our Father's heart is spelt out right here. It cannot be presented any clearer. I call it the protocol of divine favour. Protocol defined is simply this: 'A decision made by an official body of people concerning a code of conduct, etiquette or ethics for a given situation.' In other words, 'The way it is, or the way of doing things.' We have to respect the protocol when meeting royalty. There is a way of doing things concerning the game of golf. Once the protocol is agreed and set, it is unchangeable – unless the official body decides to change it. God has set a protocol for obtaining divine favour. It has been *set*! It is unchangeable and if respected and applied is guaranteed to work. It is the way into his heart. When we arrive there we find pure love – pure love and pure mercy sitting on the throne waiting to meet our need.

When I meditated on the Hebrews verse above, I realised the Holy Spirit, through the Scriptures, was giving us the route right into the centre of God's heart. As I broke the verse down, I discovered seven simple elements that if understood, believed and practised, would revolutionise our prayer life, unlock the resources of heaven and release God's ability into our disability. When I came across this amazing revelation, I felt like Indiana Jones cracking a code giving access to some amazing treasure!

Invitation

Firstly, this verse reveals God is a God of invitation. 'Let us therefore come boldly,' or as another translation puts it 'to draw near' (Amplified version). As we begin our journey to the centre of his heart, we must understand he is, first and foremost, a God of invitation. *He* is the one inviting us to come close to him at any time and with any need. He invites us to give him our burdens and cares: 'Come to Me, all you who labour and are heavy laden, and I will give you rest' (Mt. 11:28).

He invites us to take risks. Just one word given to Peter caused him to do what no other human being had done – walk on water. That word that proved to be the catalyst was 'Come'. He invites us to receive living water – 'And the Spirit and the bride say, "Come!" And let him who hears say, "Come!" And let him who thirsts come. Whoever desires, let him take of the water of life freely' (Rev. 22:17). He invites us to ask for what seems impossible. 'If you then, being evil, know how to give good gifts to your children, how much more will your Father who is in heaven give good things to those who ask Him!' (Mt. 7:11). God is like a very powerful magnet. Get into his magnetic field, and feel the pull. Some of you need to turn your theological magnets around and be drawn to him, not repelled from him.

Attitude

The second element in our journey into the presence of God is concerning our attitude. Not only does he exhort us to come, but he tells us how to come – fearlessly, confidently and boldly. God actually wants us to enter his presence much like the way my son entered mine; fearlessly, not apologetically, confident not cringing, boldly not bashful. You don't have to be shy with God. But in order to come with this attitude, the next element has to be clearly understood – location.

Location

It is one thing to hear the word 'come', but the difference between entering with or without fear is in knowing where you're being invited. Many people sit outside of

God's presence much like people sitting in a dentist's waiting room. It matters not how soft or welcoming the dentist's voice is inviting you in. What lies beyond that door does not infuse boldness or confidence or fearlessness. In fact it's totally the opposite. In order to walk into God's presence with boldness and full of anticipation, you must understand *where* he is inviting you to come. You must know what lies beyond the door. God clearly leaves us in no doubt. We are being invited to a 'throne of grace'.

Beyond the door is not some mad scientist waiting to experiment on you. There's not an electric chair to torture you, or a black-hooded hangman to execute you. Waiting for you is, instead, *a throne of favour.* You are not being invited to a throne of judgement; that's why you can come confidently and with boldness. Once inside, you are handed something that gives you access to the throne where the favour is administered; this leads to the next element.

Mercy

To receive the favour you need, you first have to 'obtain mercy'. Mercy is the access to favour. The power of mercy is in the fact that it gives you access to favour. We can all be invited to a concert, but only those holding a card saying 'Access all areas', or 'VIP' can meet the celebrity. As soon as you enter God's presence you are handed a VIP card. Written on it is mercy. With that in your possession you can go where you want without embarrassment, even up to God himself as he sits on his throne of favour.

In my book *Prepared for Greatness*, there is a whole chapter devoted to the power of mercy. Mercy in essence says, 'I restrain God from giving you what you deserve.' If the card you were holding was your 'past record', you wouldn't get near the throne of favour. If the card you were holding was 'personal holiness', you wouldn't even get near enough to see it. Hence our boldness to approach the throne of favour is not merit-based, but mercy-based.

Arrogance and boldness are two opposing attitudes. One is based on merit; the other is based on mercy. An arrogant approach is based on what I've done. An arrogant approach says, 'I am going to receive the favour I deserve.' A bold approach says, 'I'm going to receive the favour I don't deserve.' An arrogant approach says, 'It doesn't matter about my lifestyle. God understands my weaknesses. I'll stop sinning when I get stronger.' A bold approach says, 'How can God forgive me? How could I sin against such goodness? Why does God still accept me? How can I confidently walk up to his face, look into his eyes and ask for favour when I know and he knows I don't deserve it?' Then God says, 'This is the reason why. To receive favour, you first have to obtain mercy. This gives you access to all areas especially my willingness to give you what you don't deserve. That card you're holding in your hand called "Mercy" restrains me from giving you what you really deserve.'

There were a number of people in the Gospels who had justifiable reasons not to come boldly to receive favour. But with the blood-red card of mercy in their hands, they did, and received the favour they desired.

The woman who had haemorrhaged for 12 years (see Mt. 9:20–22), according to Jewish law, had to remain housebound. Her medical condition made her unclean. Not only was she unclean, but everything she touched became unclean. She fought against her own sense of unworthiness, the derogatory comments of others and the size of the crowd but with her red card of mercy in her hand she pushed through and received favour. In fact, out of the thousands touching Jesus that day, only she had obtained access to his grace. She first obtained mercy to find favour.

The Syro-Phoenician woman who came for favour for her sick daughter was not even put off by being called a dog (see Mk. 7:24–29). She didn't attempt to justify her position; she simply held up the red card of mercy and received favour. Blind Bartimaus reached out as Jesus was passing by to receive favour to eradicate his blindness. He was told to 'shut up, be silent, you're a beggar, you're not worth it'; but holding up the red card – 'Jesus, Son of David, have mercy on me!' – he stopped Jesus in his tracks and received his healing (see Mk. 10:46–52). A prostitute gatecrashed a religious gathering, threw herself down at Jesus' feet and washed them with her tears of gratitude. She had been ostracised culturally, criticised religiously and demoralised socially. As she did the unthinkable, touched the throne of favour, the Pharisee-filled room emitted a religious gasp. But Jesus silenced her critics by directing their attention to the red card of mercy she was holding. While the religious audience were appealing to their rights and her wrongs, she simply appealed to mercy that gave her the access she needed to favour (see Lk. 7:37–50). Yes, I am guilty but mercy restrains God from giving me what I deserve, allowing me to reach for the undeserved blessing of favour that can save my life. Mercy and grace work together in partnership to make sure we get blessed.

Destination

With mercy now obtained we head towards our destination. To 'find favour', we very often spend so much time formulating endless religious prayers while in the presence of God, that we forget why we came in the first place.

My wife says to me, 'Ray, go into the garage and bring me a frozen pizza from the freezer.' I get to the garage, my thoughts preoccupied with everything but the pizza, and return to my wife empty-handed. That's how we are on entering the presence of God. We accept the invitation, we'll come with the right attitude, we're not afraid, we hold the red card of mercy giving us access to the throne of favour – then we leave, forgetting why we came in the first place. We've come for favour! We've come for undeserved blessing, remember?

We gain access through obtaining mercy, walk right up to the throne of favour and God says, 'Yes, what is it? What do you need?' We stand there stuttering or mumbling something that is incoherent or 'Well, I don't really know, I just wanted to see the throne.'

When God invites us into his presence, he expects us to be present also. Before a worship service at one of our morning services, the Father whispered to me, 'Ray, you pray and intercede for my presence. You ask me to be amongst you as a congregation, but often I'm present but you are not.'

Imagine pestering someone to come and visit you. You nag them for months. They finally fit it into their schedule and turn up at your house at the prearranged date and time, only to find a note pinned to the front door: 'Sorry I missed you. Gone away for a few days. Key under the mat – let yourself in!' Not only is it one of the most disrespectful things you could do, but a sure way of losing a friend. Thank God he is not that easily offended. He keeps coming back even though often to find we are still not present. He loves being with us. We should at least show him the respect he deserves by being present when he is present. Are our minds thinking about the day's activities after the service is over or are we distracted by the worry of upcoming confrontations or are we just thinking, 'How much longer are they going to sing this song!'? The next time a friend comes to see you, in the middle of the conversation call someone on your mobile phone, turn on the TV and completely ignore them, or pick up a book and begin to read. After a few minutes, glance up and study the expression on their face. Then you will begin to understand how sometimes we treat God.

When God invites us into his presence and gives us mercy to find favour, he expects us to be specific. The lame man who lay beside the pool of Bethesda for 38 years (see Jn. 5:1–15) was asked a seemingly ridiculous question by Jesus: 'Do you want to be made well?' Jesus wanted a response. Do we get a kick simply from the spiritual experience of getting into God's presence, or have we come for a reason? Why did Jesus ask such a question of this man who was obviously aware of his need? Jesus was appealing to his *desire*. Amazingly, there are people in desperate need standing before the throne of grace who want to stay as they are! That question was packed with divine intention: 'Do you want to stay that way because you think your case is just too hopeless, or do you believe that I can help you?' It's one thing to stand at the throne of favour but it's another thing to *want* that favour ... which leads onto the next element.

Motive

You are there because you have a need and he has the ability to help you. He has not invited you into his throne room to embarrass you, trick you, punish you or destroy you. The Bible says that God is essentially a helper, not a hinderer. It is Satan's nature to hinder, it's God's nature to help. He is 'A very present help in trouble' (Ps. 46:1).

'For He Himself has said, "I will never leave you nor forsake you." So we may boldly say: "The LORD is my helper; I will not fear. What can man do to me?"' (Heb. 13:5b,6); '... the Spirit also helps in our weaknesses' (Rom.

8:26a); 'Fear not, for I am with you; Be not dismayed, for I am your God. I will strengthen you, Yes, I will *help* you, I will uphold you ...' (Is. 41:10, my italics).

Draw near to the throne of favour boldly to obtain mercy, to find favour to *help*. He is here to help you, not harass you!

Circumstance

Finally, we come to the last element that will help you understand what you'll discover when you arrive at the centre of his heart. It is 'circumstance'. He is there to help you, *in your time of need*. Favour is not a badge to display your merit – it is a gift to display his mercy. His favour is designed for, and meets, any need. Millions have stood before that throne over the centuries. Millions stand before that throne every day with needs ranging from terminal cancer to toothache, from bereavement to bankruptcy. There is no checklist before the throne as to the availability of favour for a specific need. God's throne of favour is not like the kind of store where the catalogue displays what's available but the storeroom computes 'unavailable'.

Finally ...

What area of your life needs help? If his favour can help stop a 12-year haemorrhage, fill a boat with fish, cause a man to walk on water, raise a man from the dead, what's stopping you from coming before the throne of favour with boldness to obtain mercy to find favour to help you in *your* time of need?

What a place! The centre of God's heart!

See you there.

13

The Private Heart

Recently, I was asked to write an article for a local secular magazine on the subject 'What's Christmas all about?' In my mind I waded through the usual approach of shepherds, wise men and stables. I meditated on the incredible, unexplainable miracle of God becoming flesh, the overwhelming truth of God's unprejudiced love, causing him to empty heaven of its greatest treasure and himself of his deepest joy. I contemplated and, as a result, rejoiced in all the benefits I have received as a human being, because of that selfless act of giving. Then in the midst of all these choices of themes to write about, I realised I was looking at the meaning of Christmas from the wrong perspective. The question which rarely gets asked is 'What does Christmas mean to *God*?'

How would you feel standing outside a bed and breakfast on Christmas Eve, hungry and tired after travelling hundreds of miles in the back of a truck, with your wife ready to give birth to your first child ... and the door is shut in your face? 'No room here, mate, but we do have a garage at the back you can use … oh and by the way, make sure you don't disturb our dogs and pet rabbits, they get a bit nervous around strangers.' As you pause, trying to analyse your emotions in such a predicament, you're getting close to understanding just how we treated our God when he turned up at humanity's doorstep, 2,000 years ago.

We often evaluate Christmas from our perspective but have you ever stopped to see it from God's? To us, the festive season is about gifts given and received; to him it's about rejection. John 1:11 tells us 'He came to His own, and His own did not receive Him.' Isaiah, in that great prophetic chapter, said: 'He is despised and *rejected* by men, A Man of sorrows and acquainted with grief. And we hid, as it were, our faces from Him; He was despised, and we did not esteem Him' (Is. 53:3).

He was rejected that first Christmas by people he simply wanted to love. And 2,000 years on, we're still doing it. Jesus, God in the flesh, was rejected at his birth. He was then thrown out of the town where he had lived for 30 years simply because he declared his intention to heal their sick, deliver their captives and preach hope to the suicidal. He was betrayed and forsaken by a group of guys he had spent three years pouring his experience into and finally, at the end of his brief life on earth, he was handed over by his own countrymen to be skewered on a Roman torture pole, as the final emphatic statement from a world that sneered: 'Why did you bother to come?'

Rejection is the crux of Christmas, if you see it through God's eyes. We verbalise our criticism of God based on the perception that we're dealing with an angry vindicator with bony pointed fingers of judgement aimed in our direction. But that picture doesn't fit the passion of Christ, where God was shown to die with open arms. If anyone is to be blamed for fist-shaking it should be us, not God. There are many who may not agree with what I am about to say, but from my observation as a minister, a strong conviction has planted itself in my heart and saddened it. Millions raise their fist with the followers of Darwin and say, 'God, you didn't do what you said you did. We came from apes not Adam. Who needs you? We all evolved quite nicely on our own without you, thank you.' And we reject him as Creator.

Multitudes watch Dan Brown's blockbuster, *The Da Vinci Code*, and say: 'You are not who you say you are, you had sex with a prostitute.' Divine, who are you kidding? And the rejection continues! And what about the atheist? The ultimate rejecter who has no need to shake his fist at God? How can you shake your fist at someone who is not there?

It's like the story I heard[20] concerning a scientist who challenges God: 'We can do most anything, God; anything you can do, we can do.' God says, 'OK, here is the challenge; let us make a man.' 'OK,' says the scientist, 'I'll go first.' And he reaches down and picks up a handful of dust. 'No, no,' says God. 'You make your own dust!' The lesson was learned.

We reject him in our schools. Children ask their teachers, 'Why did God call his Son after a swear word?' It seems there is an all-out aversion to the exposure of our children and teenagers to anything Christian, under the premise we're bending their minds. Wearing a cross or a crucifix suddenly appears unacceptable, although members of other faiths are allowed to wear articles displaying their religion. Recently, a British Airways worker was told she could not prominently wear her tiny cross, the symbol of her faith; this caused a huge uproar and as a result, newspapers published valid comments from many people, including leading churchmen.

The world's media celebrates the success of the Harry Potter films – films that introduce children to the occult, witchcraft and sorcery – but make all manner of criticisms against the *Chronicles of Narnia*, C.S. Lewis's brilliant adaptation of the fundamental truths of our faith, some to the point of being downright offensive to the Christian. Isaiah was way beyond his time; he had never read these remarks when he profoundly and prophetically stated that Jesus would be rejected.

Sometimes rejection of Christ can also be tasted in the way blame is firmly placed at his feet for every tragedy, either through nature or through war. Anne Graham, one of Billy Graham's daughters, was being interviewed on an American TV chat show and was asked how God could allow hurricane Katrina – a devastating hurricane that levelled the city of New Orleans, and took the lives of hundreds in 2005. Her answer was both thought-provoking and brilliantly relevant. She said she believed God is deeply saddened, but for years we've been telling him to get out of our schools, out of our government, and out of our lives. Being the gentleman that he is, he has calmly backed out. When we demand he leaves us alone, how then can we demand God give us his protection and blessing?

I was very encouraged and challenged by the words of Dr John Sentamu, when newly inaugurated as Archbishop of York. He noted that Christians in the west have largely rejected what it actually means to be a disciple of the Lord Jesus; Sentamu said that the vast majority of western Christians are just members of churches, fillers of pews, singers of hymns, tasters of sermons, and readers of the Bible.

We criticise the innkeeper, who refused entry to the pregnant virgin. We criticise Judas for his mercenary spirit, which led to Jesus' arrest and death. We criticise Pilate for his spineless attempt to avoid taking a personal responsibility regarding Jesus. We criticise the mob for being easily swayed by the convictions of others. But are we not just as guilty of the same shortcomings? The only difference is that we can hide ours from the gaze of others because of God's gift to us of personal sovereignty. But when he calls us to dine with him in the privacy of our own hearts, our hypocrisy, double standards and compromise are lovingly challenged. We begin to empathise with Peter and know exactly what he felt like as Jesus took him on a journey to the centre of his heart over a divinely prepared breakfast by the sea (see Jn. 21:15–19). On his private cardio excursion, Jesus had Peter stop at three stations. Perhaps in days past, Peter had whizzed passed them refusing to stop, maybe for fear of what he would find there.

Responsibility

The station of responsibility was Peter's first stop. And as he stepped off the train, in big bold letters over the station entrance were these words: 'Do you?' This was no time to measure his failure with others, building a defence based on comparison. This was no time to blow out another's candle so his shone brighter. Peter had to face and answer Jesus honestly, if he was to carry the responsibility of feeding his Saviour's sheep, and taking the gospel to the world.

Relationship

Station number two was relationship. Firstly, his personal relationship with Jesus had to be established and secondly, the focus and priority of his love. Jesus did not ask Peter 'Do you love the ministry?' because he knew there would be days when he would want to leave it. He did not ask him 'Do you love my sheep?' because he knew there would be days when, through frustration, he would want to eat them! Jesus took Peter on a journey to the centre of his heart to settle the fundamental question which is the bedrock of fulfilled destiny: 'Do you love *me*?'

Peter had to pass the love test. Not the theological test, success test, or gifting test. Jesus knew if Peter was to go all the way to a martyr's death, the basis for his service would have to go beyond prestige, money or status. Jesus knew for Peter to go where he wouldn't want to go, submit to what he didn't want to submit to, pay a price he certainly *naturally* wouldn't want to pay, he had to pass the love test.

The reason why many give up and fail to finish their course is found right here at the station of relationship. Many people fail to relate to Jesus based on love; their relationship is based on fear of judgement, and guilt. That's why we, too, will take the journey with Jesus to the centre of our heart, in order for this issue to be cemented.

In the very moving blockbuster *Saving Private Ryan*, Tom Hanks plays the part of an officer in charge of a group of men assigned to find a soldier called Ryan. Ryan's three brothers, unknown to him, had already been killed on the battlefield. The government felt the death of the last son would be a burden the mother would not be able to take. So in order to save her more pain, the last remaining son, Ryan, had to be found and brought home. Most of the heroic group of men assigned to the mission died in the attempt, including the officer played by Tom Hanks.

In the final scene, Hank's character is dying, with Ryan, now found, kneeling by his side. Ryan stoops closer to hear the last words of his human saviour, and for the rest of his life, they will live with him and he with them. With his dying breath, Hank's character whispers that Ryan must 'earn' what has been done for him. In other words, 'Don't let our sacrifice have been in vain. Because of what we've done for you, make sure the rest of your life is spent earning the price paid for you to live it.' How different it would have been for Ryan if the last words were, 'Appreciate this.' The difference between 'earn' and 'appreciate' is the difference between living a life of guilt or gratitude. How many Christians live with a continual sense of guilt because they feel they have to earn the price paid for them at Calvary? Do you feel guilty if you miss your daily devotions? Do you feel God loves you more when you've performed well? Do you feel obligated to prove yourself more faithful after you've been forgiven for some failure or sin? If the answer to these questions is yes, you have failed the love test. Your relationship with Jesus is based on guilt not gratitude, fear not love, law not grace, and judgement not forgiveness.

Philip Yancey in *What's so Amazing about Grace?* stated: 'Can anyone fulfil the greatest commandment, to love God from fear of punishment? Love can never be forced; it flows out of fullness not fear.' No amount of self-effort can change the heart. No human tradition has the power to produce true spirituality; no degree of separation can shield us from sin. No amount of moral uprightness can produce righteousness. Put whatever name you want to 'religion' – Islam, Catholicism, Protestantism or Judaism – flesh will never get you to God, God must get to us. The remedy to religion is relationship. Be warned against the practise of embracing grace for salvation and rejecting it for sanctification. 'Do you love me?' is the most simple but important question Jesus will ever ask us. How we answer is imperative to the rest of our lives.

Replacement

The third station Peter visited as Jesus took him on a journey to the centre of his heart was 'Replacement': 'Do you love Me *more than these*?' (my italics). Jesus can do little with a disciple whose heart is divided. How sad it would be if a bride stood ready to take her vows, giving herself in lifelong commitment to someone, while her heart was longing for someone else. Jesus was asking Peter, and indirectly every one of us: 'Is there anything or anyone in your life that takes my place?' Not only did Jesus ask for his whole heart, but he expected Peter to bury the competition. Unbelievers forfeit God's best for their lives through rejection. A believer does the same through replacement.

Why does God say things like 'You shall have no other gods before me' (Ex. 20:3, NIV) or 'Love the Lord your God with all your heart and with all your soul and with all your mind and with all your strength' (Mk. 12:30, NIV) or '… seek first the kingdom of God …' (Mt. 6:33). It is not to stroke his ego or manipulate our love. It is to save us from the disappointment of misdirected affection, or the disappointment that comes as a result of putting something or someone in the place in our lives where only God should be. It wasn't enough for Peter to pass the love test; he also had to pass the 'replacement test' – 'more than these'. Jesus could have been referring to his fishing business, his friends, who knows what? But I do know this. As Jesus takes us to the centre of our heart, we will have to stop at the station of replacement where we will be confronted with the same question. 'Is there anyone or anything that has replaced me at the centre of your life?'

We have still not learned from our first parents, Adam and Eve. If they had focused their faith and affection on God, they would have lived as he intended, complete and contented. They chose to replace God with an alternative and the rest, as they say, is history. The powerful searching encounter between Jesus and a rich young ruler can also help us reorder our priorities. Here's how Jesus took this young man on a journey to the centre of his heart.

Now as He was going out on the road, one came running, knelt before Him, and asked Him, 'Good Teacher, what shall I do that I may inherit eternal life?' So Jesus said to him, 'Why do you call Me good? No one is good but One, that is, God. You know the commandments: "Do not commit adultery," "Do not murder," "Do not steal," "Do not bear false witness," "Do not defraud," "Honour your father and your mother."' And he answered and said to Him, 'Teacher, all these things I have kept from my youth.' Then Jesus, looking at him, loved him, and said to him, 'One thing you lack: Go your way, sell whatever you have and give to the poor, and you will have treasure in heaven; and come, take up the cross, and follow Me.' But he was sad at this word, and went away sorrowful, for he had great possessions (Mk. 10:17–22).

This young man was rich, he was respected, he was religious and he also had a revelation of who Jesus was. However, with all this going for him, after his encounter with Jesus, he went away sad. Why? His love for money had replaced his love for God. The source of this young man's sadness was not rejection but replacement. Combined with his unwillingness to kick the usurper off the throne of his heart would be the knowledge that life would never be fulfilling. Could it be the seasons of sadness in your life though you are a Christian, are the same? Someone or something has replaced God at the centre of your life. Jesus points out, on various occasions, that the subtlety of replacement lies in the fact that these things that compete for the throne of your life are deceptively legitimate. He warns against spouse replacement, family replacement, work replacement and a whole list of others. Check out Matthew 10:34–39; 19:29; Luke 14:25–27.

Jesus is not asking us to be unloving towards our spouse, or disrespectful towards our parents or even irresponsible concerning money, possessions or work. He is simply warning us of the consequences of them replacing him as a priority in our life. When exhorting us to 'hate our father and mother', he is just asking us to relinquish our claim to people and things in our lives, and place them at his disposal. The word 'hate' does not mean rejection of them, but renouncement of ownership. Jesus, in his classic sermon delivered from a mountain-top, explains why it is so important to get divinely centred: 'Wherever you place your highest values, whatever is at your centre, you will be motivated to propel your life in that direction.' (See Mt. 6:21.)

Think on these things; there may be some adjustments that have to be made in order for you to enjoy your Christian life to the max. Perhaps you have been trying to meditate your sadness away instead of being honest about the priorities of your heart.

Finally ...

Some time ago, I was preaching in a small church in the north of England. I was using Revelation 3:20 as my text: 'Behold, I stand at the door and knock. If anyone hears My voice and opens the door, I will come in to him and dine with him, and he with Me.' My remarks were directed towards Christians who were attempting to live their lives with Jesus on the outside. The emphasis of the message was not on our irresponsibility or on the stupidity of thinking it's possible, but on the passionate plea of our Saviour as he seeks to take his rightful place at the centre of our lives. At the end of the message, I asked people to come forward for prayer. Many came, but my heart reached out to one particular teenage girl who seemed to be carrying the weight of the world upon her shoulders.

As I looked at her expressionless face, out of my mouth came these words: 'Young lady, I feel God is asking you to take the "Do not disturb" sign down from the door of your room.' She lifted her head, her eyes as wide as saucers, then as if an explosion had taken place inside her, her once expressionless face turned into a picture of tearful joy. Tears rolled copiously down her face; she seemed uncontrollable. A man ran over to her, put his arms around her to comfort her. Later, I learned he was her father and pastor of the church. When I inquired as to the intensity of his daughter's reaction to those words, he said, 'My daughter has been suffering with depression. She has been desperately longing for God to help her. Preachers come and preach about the love of God, and his desire to live at the centre of our lives. Although my daughter longs to embrace Jesus in unconditional surrender, she doesn't really believe deep down he wants to embrace her. On her bedroom door, she has placed a sign, "Do not disturb. Depressed person inside." When you spoke those words, she knew it was a direct attempt by Jesus to gain entrance through the door of her heart. At that moment, she knew he cared. At that moment, she knew he loved her. She knew the problem was not his rejection of her but her replacement of him. She knew it wasn't a question of his love for her, but her refusal to accept it.'

It's time to take down the 'Do not disturb' signs from the door of your heart. It's time to abandon our self-imposed privacy, and throw the doors wide open to the best friend we will ever have. If you are reading these words, still unable to truly embrace as a reality his personal acceptance and love for you, then God wants you to take that journey to the centre of his heart. The discovery on arrival will banish all doubt once and for all about just how loved you are.

Prayer

Do you want to know God?

Dear God,

I ask you to forgive me for all my sins. I believe that Jesus Christ is your son. I receive Jesus into my life as Lord and Saviour.   AMEN.

If you found yourself praying this prayer, please don't hesitate to contact us and we can help you find a good church. Please contact us on *admin@kings-church.org.uk.*

End Notes

1 Jules Verne, *Journey to the Centre of the Earth* (London: Penguin Books Ltd., 1994).
2 Ray Bevan, *Prepared for Greatness* (Newport, South Wales: Rayla Press, 2001).
3 Francis Frangipane, *The Power of One Christ-like Life* (New Kensington: Whittaker House, 2000).
4 F.B. Meyer, Charles Spurgeon and Billy Graham quotes – every effort has been made to find the source of all quoted material whilst producing this book but some has remained unfound.
5 Source unknown.
6 Rick Warren, *The Purpose Driven Life* (Grand Rapids, MI: Zondervan, 2002).
7 Joyce Meyer, *Approval Addiction* (New York: Warner Faith, 2005).
8 Philip Yancey, *What's so Amazing about Grace?* (Grand Rapids, MI: Zondervan, 1997).
9 The set of teaching CDs, 'Burying the Lies about Singleness' is available from www.kings-church.org.uk.
10 I first read this story in Ray Comfort, *The Mantle of the Harlot* (Bell Flower, California: Living Waters Publications, 1992).

11 Source unknown.
12 Max Lucado, *It's Not About Me* (Brentwood, Tennessee: Integrity Publishers, 2004).
13 My thanks to Francis Frangipane, on whose work these ideas are based.
14 Brian McLaren, *A New Kind of Christian* (San Francisco, CA: Jossey-Boss, a Wiley imprint, 2001).
15 Ray Comfort, *The Mantle of the Harlot* (Bell Flower, California: Living Waters Publications, 1992). The teaching I share here is based on his original thought.
16 Source unknown.
17 Source unknown.
18 Steve Chalke and Alan Mann, *The Lost Message of Jesus* (Grand Rapids, MI: Zondervan, 2004).
19 Original source of this story unknown.
20 Source unknown.

Prepared for Greatness

Ray Bevan

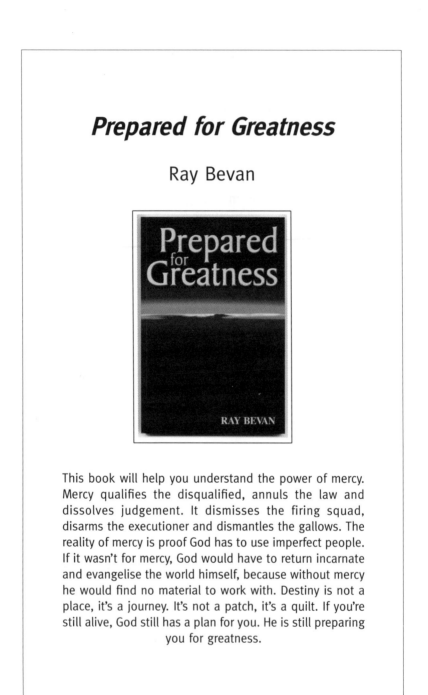

This book will help you understand the power of mercy. Mercy qualifies the disqualified, annuls the law and dissolves judgement. It dismisses the firing squad, disarms the executioner and dismantles the gallows. The reality of mercy is proof God has to use imperfect people. If it wasn't for mercy, God would have to return incarnate and evangelise the world himself, because without mercy he would find no material to work with. Destiny is not a place, it's a journey. It's not a patch, it's a quilt. If you're still alive, God still has a plan for you. He is still preparing you for greatness.